O give thanks

O give thanks
that spring will always come
to make the heart leap,
that your winter ear remembers
a summer song,
and autumn colours return
to the jaded eye.

O make song
for lucid air of morning,
bright blood's beating
life's flow deep and swift,
a kingdom of joy and awe
for us to dwell in.

O be glad
for eye and tongue
to see and taste
the common of our days.

Chaim Stern

(*The Gates of Prayer: The New Union Prayerbook*
© Central Conference of American Rabbis)

For Brendan and Nunci
with love

Some put their trust in chariots or horses,
But we in the name of the LORD, our God.
Psalm 20:7, *Revised Grail Psalter*

HEARERS OF THE
WORD

PRAYING & EXPLORING THE READINGS
ADVENT & CHRISTMAS: YEAR C

KIERAN J O'MAHONY OSA

Messenger Publications,
37 Leeson Place, Dublin D02 E5V0
www.messenger.ie

Table of Contents

Introduction

As regular readers will notice, the *Hearers of the Word* books give due weight to the contexts of events and the context of writing. Something similar may be said of the series itself. What is happening now shapes the way we hear the living word. Worldwide, the effect of the pandemic can hardly be overstated. Like Jacob at the Jabbok in Genesis 32:22–32, we all carry the marks of the struggle. We know this at many levels, including at the spiritual level of our lives.

More locally, the context of the Irish Church has been one of evident decline, punctuated by the unpredictable aftershocks of our dark past. Derek Scally's book *The Best Catholics in the World*,[1] traces that past, both remote and recent. Scally regrets, in particular, the absence of almost any adult education in the faith, leaving many who still hang in there without a lifeline to make sense of it all. So far, you might think, so bleak. But there is also hope. Two dimensions come to mind: the proposed national synod and the Gospel according to Luke, the gospel for the current year.

It is really good news that the Irish Catholic Church has finally begun a journey towards a national synod or assembly. It is certainly time to take stock. The word synod is of relatively new currency for us, although our sister church, the Church of Ireland, has a rich and deep history of synodal government. In the New Testament, the word *synodia* occurs once, in the Gospel of Luke. In chapter 2, the twelve-year-old Jesus has somehow been overlooked, as the family returns to Nazareth: *Assuming that he was in the group of travellers, they went a day's journey* (Luke 2:44).

1   Derek Scally, *The Best Catholics in the Word. The Irish, the Church and the End of a Special Relationship*, Milton Keynes: Penguin Sandycove, 2021.

The Greek for the 'group of travellers' is *synodia*. So, a synod means to make a journey together and may involve getting lost for a time! The image is eloquent and in tune with the times.

In his gospel, Luke has many journeys, closing with the remarkable tableau of the disciples on the road to Emmaus. The Acts too is teeming with travel tales, as we witness the Christian community slowly coming to birth. The history is idealised, of course, but even Luke cannot hide the fact that not all was sunshine and light. This is evident in several stories, such as the conflict over circumcision or the disturbing tale of Annas and Sapphira. All the same, in the Acts of the Apostles, there is a remarkable energy and an enviable vitality. I would pick out three qualities of the early Church: they had something to say, many were really gifted people, such as Paul himself, and *they listened to and were guided by the Spirit*. Such listening to the Spirit will have to be part of our synodal process into the future.

It is a grace that we have the Gospel of Luke and the Acts to accompany us this liturgical year. If someone were to ask, where in the New Testament would you find the best teaching on prayer, I would unhesitatingly respond that it is to be found in three places: in the undisputed letters of Paul, in the Gospel of John and in the double volume of Luke–Acts. It is not accidental that all three sets of writings also have the best teaching on the Holy Spirit and on joy. A recovery of energy and vitality can come only from prayer, grounded in the experience of the Spirit and felt in joyful discipleship. Such a regeneration of hope can have no other genesis than the Word of God.

Hope cannot be a cheap grace, however. Scottish writer Ali Smith speaks about the difference between hope and optimism, as follows:

> Optimism and hope aren't the same: optimism's a state we can consciously bring about; hope … there's nothing bunny rabbit or self-indulgent or sparkly about it, because its obverse is despair. Hope is a tightrope across a ravine between a here and a there, and that tightrope's as sharp as a knife blade.[2]

As we make our way from 'a here' to 'a there' – a balancing act if ever there was one – let us 'put on the breastplate of faith and love, and for

2   Ali Smith, Interview with Kate Kellaway in *The Guardian*, 1 May 2021.

a helmet the hope of salvation' (1 Thessalonians 5:8). As St Paul says elsewhere, 'Hope does not disappoint us, because God's love has been poured into our hearts through the Holy Spirit that has been given to us' (Romans 5:5). May the sun rise on us, as it rose on Jacob (Genesis 32:31).

Thanks as always to my confrère John Byrne OSA, the source for nearly all the Pointers for Prayer on the gospel readings. Sincere thanks, too, to Messenger Publications for staying with the project in difficult times for book publishers.

Chapter 1

Advent 1C

Thought for the day

If you were to wish people a happy new year today, they would in all probability find it awkward. Nevertheless, we do start a new Christian year with the season of Advent. The changing seasons remind us of different aspects of being Christian, one of which is the conviction that we may always begin again and start new. Last Sunday we looked back and today we look forward: What are *my* hopes for the coming Christian year? How am I now? How would I like to be, as a believer, this time next year? What steps will I take to make that a reality?

Prayer

O God, we believe that your mercies are new every morning and that your faithfulness is abundant. Come to our help as we start afresh our path of discipleship in this season of longing and hope. We make our prayer through Christ our Lord. Amen.

🌿 Gospel 🌿

Lk 21:25 [Jesus said:] 'There will be signs in the sun, the moon, and the stars, and on the earth distress among nations confused by the roaring of the sea and the waves. [26] People will faint from fear and foreboding of what is coming upon the world, for the powers of the heavens will be shaken. [27] Then they will see "the Son of Man coming in a cloud" with power and great glory. [28] Now when these things begin to take place, stand up and raise your heads, because your redemption is drawing near.'

29 Then he told them a parable: 'Look at the fig tree and all the trees; 30 as soon as they sprout leaves you can see for yourselves and know that summer is already near. 31 So also, when you see these things taking place, you know that the kingdom of God is near. 32 Truly I tell you, this generation will not pass away until all things have taken place. 33 Heaven and earth will pass away, but my words will not pass away.

34 'Be on guard so that your hearts are not weighed down with dissipation and drunkenness and the worries of this life, and that day catch you unexpectedly, 35 like a trap. For it will come upon all who live on the face of the whole earth. 36 Be alert at all times, praying that you may have the strength to escape all these things that will take place, and to stand before the Son of Man.'

Initial observations

Advent is a clarion call to renew once more, in a conscious and personal fashion, our engagement with the Good News. The two gospel passages that open Advent portray two sides of the Christian vision. Vv. 25–28, the vision of the end, constitute a rereading of traditional material from Mark 13, which was written down during a time of persecution. Behind the dramatic – lurid? – language lies a foundational faith conviction: there is a pattern and a purpose to life. The imposing immediacy of the times, with the impression of that being all there is, is challenged by Christian faith and hope. The second paragraph, vv. 34–36, responds to the spontaneous question, if this is the case, then how should we act in the present? The answer is twofold: watchfulness and prayer. (The parable of the fig tree, which bridges the passages, is not given in the lectionary – a pity, because of the great assurance given in v. 33.)

Broadly speaking, Luke portrays Jesus as a prophet, part of whose prophecy has already come to pass and part of which remains to be fulfilled. The last verse is very good news: the arrival of the Son of Man contains no fears for those faithful to prayer, in faith and in hope.

Kind of writing

As noted elsewhere, this is 'apocalyptic', a particular kind of writing that flourished from about 200 BC onwards in certain Jewish contexts. The major apocalypses in the Bible are the Book of Daniel and Revelation. Mark 13 is known as the Little Apocalypse and forms the basis for the Lucan text here.

The setting for apocalyptic is usually some situation of threat or persecution, where the very basis of the faith is under pressure. People are typically asking 'where is God in all this?' Apocalyptic writing tries to help people understand the quality of the times and how they should act accordingly. Apocalyptic writing is usually heavily symbolic, even esoteric. Nevertheless, the basic message is twofold: there is a purpose in all this, even if we cannot see it now, and we are asked to practise *endurance*, that is, faith and hope.

Luke's end-time discourse (21:5–37) unfolds in three distinct, uneven moments.

1* *The Fall of the Temple* (21:5–11)
2 The time before the Fall of the Temple (21:12–19 – an excursus)

1* *The Fall of the Temple* (21:20–24)
3 The Days of the Son of Man (21:25–37)

Our excerpt, therefore, comes from the very last part of the discourse. For the readers of Luke, Parts 1 and 2 are already past (Jerusalem had fallen etc.). The factual fulfilment of the prediction strengthens our faith in Jesus as a prophet as we listen to the words about the end of time. There is a literary pattern across 21:5–37:

A The time of the eschaton, warning not to be misled (vv. 8–9)
  B Political upheavals (v. 10)
    C Cosmic disturbances (v. 11)

D The time of testimony (which comes before all
this) (vv. 12–19)

B' Political upheavals (of which the fall of Jerusalem is
a part) (vv. 20–24)

C' Cosmic disturbances (vv. 25–26)

A' The time of the eschaton, warning to be ready (vv. 27– 36)

Old Testament background

Luke 21:26 is an allusion: For thus says the LORD of hosts: Once
again, in a little while, I will shake the heavens and the earth
and the sea and the dry land. (Haggai 2:6)

Luke 21:27 is a citation: As I watched in the night visions, I saw
one like a son of man coming with the clouds of heaven.
And he came to the Ancient One and was presented before
him. (Daniel 7:13)

Luke 21:35 is an allusion: Terror, and the pit, and the snare are
upon you, O inhabitant of the earth! (Isaiah 24:17)

New Testament foreground

The sense of high expectation for an end-time intervention by
God is found widely in the New Testament. The very preaching
of Jesus himself would be an example: 'But he said to them, "I
must proclaim the good news of the kingdom of God to the
other cities also; for I was sent for this purpose"' (Luke 4:43).

While Luke 21:25–28 is based on Mark 13:24–27, Luke 21:34–36 has
no parallel elsewhere in the gospels.

But in those days, after that suffering, the sun will be darkened,
and the moon will not give its light, and the stars will be
falling from heaven, and the powers in the heavens will be
shaken. Then they will see 'the Son of Man coming in clouds'
with great power and glory. Then he will send out the angels,
and gather his elect from the four winds, from the ends of the
earth to the ends of heaven. (Mark 13:24–27)

St Paul

> And do this because we know the time, that it is already the hour for us to awake from sleep, for our salvation is now nearer than when we became believers. The night has advanced towards dawn; the day is near. So then we must lay aside the works of darkness, and put on the weapons of light. Let us live decently as in the daytime, not in carousing and drunkenness, not in sexual immorality and sensuality, not in discord and jealousy. Instead, put on the Lord Jesus Christ, and make no provision for the flesh to arouse its desires. (Romans 13:11–14)

Brief commentary

When reading this material there are four levels to be distinguished: (i) what really happened; (ii) how this was interpreted in earliest Christianity; (iii) the continuing interpretation in Mark and Q Sayings Source; (iv) Luke's own interpretation of the preceding traditions. Luke's own reception suggests the following parameters for reading:

a. History has an end and a purpose.

b. The first generations of Christians read the terrible events of their day (e.g. the Jewish War, the destruction of Jerusalem) as signs of the end; however, *this was not the case*, as it turned out.

c. The consequent delay and reinterpretation are no excuse for complacency; courageous witness during the time of mission is still the call of all believers.

(V. 25)

The discourse broadens out from Jerusalem with the expression 'signs' and the mention of 'earth' and 'nations'. Here, the Markan tradition, which saw particular historical events as the sign of the end, is adjusted to point to cosmic signs, visible to all.

(V. 26)

The text moves from celestial signs to the reactions of those still alive, vividly portrayed. There is no mistaking the 'shock and awe' marking the end. Notice again the mention of 'world'.

(V. 27)

This is a direct citation of Daniel 7:13. Luke has prepared his readers for this – see Luke 9:26; 11:30; 12:8, 40; 17:22, 24, 26, 30; 18:8. The Son of Man is coming not with violence and vengeance; instead, it will be the very same Jesus whom we know from Luke's portrait, full of compassion and love. The proper preparation for his return is not speculation about the end, but simply repentance and loving service.

(V. 28)

At this point, Luke omits Mark: '*Then he will send out the angels, and gather his elect from the four winds, from the ends of the earth to the ends of heaven*' (Mark 13:27), and replaces that verse with consoling words of encouragement.

(Vv. 29–30)

The little parable indicates that the signs will be unmistakable and there will no need for speculation or speculative interpreters. The sprouting fig tree is a very unthreatening image: spring leading to summer.

(V. 31)

This is the clear promise that there will indeed be an end, when God brings history to its consummation.

(V. 32)

Luke takes v. 32 from Mark and he already knows that, at a literal level, it had not happened. Luke has most likely changed the reference to the very last generation, the generation that will not have passed away.

(V. 33)

Jesus is God's ultimate spokesman, and his word, like the word of God in the Hebrew Bible, abides (Isaiah 40:8; Psalm 119:89, 160). *The sum of your word is truth; and every one of your righteous ordinances endures forever* (Psalm 119:160).

(V. 34)

'Be on your guard' is a theme in Luke (12:1; 17:3; 20:46). He is really struggling against a relaxed complacency now that the end is not an imminent threat. Luke alone mentions dissipation etc., which brings the discourse very much into the present moment and the experience of the hearers. Cf. *So then let us not fall asleep as others do, but let us keep awake and be sober; for those who sleep sleep at night, and those who are drunk get drunk at night* (1 Thessalonians 5:6–7).

(V. 35)

Luke underscores the universality of these closing events. Once more, it won't be simply historical upheavals, but a cosmic, universal event.

(V. 36)

The verb used here for praying means rather more narrowly interceding, that is, prayer of petition (Luke 5:12; 8:28, 38; 9:38, 40; 10:2; 22:32). Teaching on prayer is a feature of Luke, as is his more frequent portrayal of Jesus at prayer. The discourse comes to rest on a positive and practical note.

Pointers for prayer

a) This passage can be taken as a metaphor for personal experiences when it seemed that your world was collapsing around you: plans thwarted, deep disappointment, something out of your control altering the course of your life etc. When have such experiences been a prelude to something new? Allow the dramatic language of the passage to remind you of this experience, making sure that you recognise the double movement of collapse and liberation.

b) Jesus himself is the model in this gospel story as he taught his disciples the spirituality of 'waiting in joyful hope'. What difference has watchfulness (in the sense of being watchful in prayer) made to you in facing difficult situations?

c) Advent is a time that calls us to be alert to the signs of the hidden presence of God in our world. What reminds you of this presence of God? Have there been occasions when something woke you up in an unexpected way to the presence of God in the world, for example love, beauty, nature and so forth?

Prayer

God, our saviour, you utter a word of promise and hope and hasten the day of justice and freedom, yet we live in a world forgetful of your word, our watchfulness dulled by the cares of life.

Keep us alert. Make us attentive to your word, ready to look on your Son when he comes with power and great glory. Make us holy and blameless, ready to stand secure when the day of his coming shakes the world with terror.

We ask this through him whose coming is certain, whose day draws near: your Son, Jesus Christ, who lives and reigns with you in the unity of the Holy Spirit, God, for ever and ever. Amen.

Second Reading

1 Thess 3:12 And may the Lord cause you to increase and abound in love for one another and for all, just as we do for you, [13] so that your hearts are strengthened in holiness to be blameless before our God and Father at the coming of our Lord Jesus with all his saints.

4:1 Finally then, brothers and sisters, we ask you and urge you in the Lord Jesus, that as you received instruction from us about how you must live and please God (as you are in fact living) that you do so more and more. [2] For you know what commands we gave you through the Lord Jesus.

Initial observations

This prayer and exhortation are both very suitable for the season of Advent. The text can be read in relation to the community in Thessalonica at the time of Paul and also in relation to our personal preparation for the birth of the saviour this year.

Kind of writing

1 Thessalonians is a letter, using the structural patterns of classical rhetoric.

1:1	Epistolary superscript
1:2–10	Thanksgiving/Introduction
1:9–10	Thesis in three parts
2:1–3:12	Relationships with Paul
4:1–12	Living in love and holiness
4:13–5:11	End-time issues
5:12–27	Exhortation/Conclusion
5:28	Epistolary postscript

The two paragraphs of our reading straddle two sections of the letter. 1 Thessalonians 3:12–13 – a prayer – concludes the restoration of relationships and foreshadows the topics to come in the next two sections. 1 Thessalonians 4:1–2 serves to open the topic of how to live in love and holiness in a hostile environment.

Origin of the reading

The pastoral context is primarily one of irritation and disappointment. Paul had been to Thessalonica around AD 49 and had moved on to Athens. While he was in Athens a cry for help came, but Paul himself did not return to Macedonia. Instead he sent Timothy. Upon the latter's return, Paul is aware that there is some fence-mending to be done. 1 Thessalonians 2–3 constitutes an attempt to restore the affection and esteem of the Thessalonians for Paul.

Apart from this immediate issue with their founder, the Thessalonians also have a number of urgent questions. How do we live in the hostile environment of the empire and emperor worship? What about the dead? When will the end be?

While almost certainly the first Christian document to come down to us and the first surviving letter of St Paul, 1 Thessalonians is a mature document, reflecting Paul's experience of some fifteen years of proclamation in Syria and Cilicia.

Related passages

And you became imitators of us and of the Lord, when you received the message with joy that comes from the Holy Spirit, despite great affliction. As a result you became an example to all the believers in Macedonia and in Achaia. For from you the message of the Lord has echoed forth not just in Macedonia and Achaia, but in every place reports of your faith in God have spread, so that we do not need to say anything. For people everywhere report how you welcomed us and how you turned to God from idols to serve the living and true God and to wait for his Son from heaven, whom he raised from the dead, Jesus our deliverer from the coming wrath. (1 Thessalonians 1:6–10)

Now on the topic of brotherly love you have no need for anyone to write you, for you yourselves are taught by God to love one another. And indeed you are practising it towards all the brothers and sisters in all of Macedonia. But we urge you, brothers and sisters, to do so more and more, to aspire to lead a quiet life, to attend to your own business, and to work with your own hands, as we commanded you. In this way you will live a decent life before outsiders and not be in need. (1 Thessalonians 4:9–12)

Owe no one anything, except to love one another, for the one who loves his neighbour has fulfilled the law. For the commandments, 'Do not commit adultery, do not murder, do not steal, do not covet' (and if there is any other commandment) are summed up in this, 'Love your neighbour as yourself.' Love does no wrong to a neighbour. Therefore love is the fulfilment of the law. (Romans 13:8–10)

Brief commentary

Ch. 3 (V. 12)

Paul engages his hearers in a prayer as he concludes the careful restoration of affection between him and the Thessalonian Christians. They had doubted his apparent love for them and now he prays that they may abound in love for each other and for all – not excluding Paul himself! Elsewhere, Paul can unabashedly evoke his hearers' indebtedness to himself: *Now as you excel in everything – in faith, in speech, in knowledge, in utmost eagerness, and in our love for you – so we want you to excel also in this generous undertaking* (2 Corinthians 8:7).

(V. 13)

Earlier in the letter, Paul outlined the three topics – relationships, holiness and hope – in 1 Thessalonians 1:9–10. He is now about to take up the remaining issues in the next two sections (1 Thessalonians 4:1–12; 4:13–5:11). The mention here resumes the topics after the long and emotionally intense restoration of affection in 1 Thessalonians 2:1–3:12.

Ch. 4 (V. 1)

It might seem that Paul resembles the preacher here, inserting 'finally' long before the end! However, in Greek, *loipon* has a range of meanings: *beyond that, in addition, finally*. 'Furthermore' would be a good version in context. The combination of *indicative* (you are doing) with *imperative* (do so more and more) is very Pauline. He affirms before he exhorts – a lesson for us all.

(V. 2)

Given the way the lectionary cuts off here, the final sentence feels inevitably incomplete. We wonder what were the instructions and so forth (it turns out that Paul is dealing chiefly with sexual ethics). The *Revised Common Lectionary* does a better job in choosing 1 Thessalonians 3:9–13 as the reading.

Pointers for prayer

a) To be 'abounding in love' sounds good but is quite a challenge in the real world. From whom have I received such love? To whom do I show it?

b) Conversion – that deep change of heart and mind and life – is never done and dusted, but on the contrary the task of a lifetime. In computer language, 'under construction'. It is no harm to ask, Where do I find myself in the present moment?

Prayer

We need, O God, the strength that comes from you, if we are to be true followers of Jesus your Son. As we attend to his word, send your Spirit into our hearts that we may believe what we hear and put into practice what we believe and be your children both in name and in fact. Through Christ our Lord. Amen.

🌿 First Reading 🌿

Jer 33:14 The days are surely coming, says the LORD, when I will fulfil the promise I made to the house of Israel and the house of Judah. ¹⁵ In those days and at that time I will cause a righteous Branch to spring up for David; and he shall execute justice and righteousness in the land. ¹⁶ In those days Judah will be saved and Jerusalem will live in safety. And this is the name by which it will be called: 'The LORD is our righteousness'.

Initial observations

Jeremiah's ministry encompassed the traumatic Babylonian Exile. He was a key figure in the interpretation of that disaster and, in spite of his reputation ('jeremiads'), he was also part of the awakening of hope. This is reflected in today's reading, promising restoration and reconstruction.

The combination of penetrating blame and uplifting healing may be just what the Church stands in need of today.

Kind of writing

Jeremiah 33:14–26 is a difficult passage as a whole. It promises a future for both Levitical priests and a Davidic king. A comparable ideology may be found in Sirach 45 (see below). In both, the covenant with Aaron is given priority over the covenant with David.

Such prioritising tells us a good deal about the writers and issues at the time of writing. However, even though the passage as a whole presents challenges, the verses chosen in the lectionary are clear enough.

Origin of the reading

Along with Isaiah and Ezekiel, Jeremiah is one of the major prophets. The book we now have is an extraordinary literary and theological achievement. As we can see below from the structure, the first part of the book re-enacts the dismantling of tribal structures, cultic institutions and symbolic systems. The telling is full of haunting imagery and deep feeling. A whole way of being has simply collapsed. How to cope with the massive wreckage of a cherished world?

The second part of the book is devoted to a deep theology of suffering as the basis for the construction of new possibilities and restoration after the immense pain of deportation and exile. Given our situation of cultural 'exile' at the moment, we have much to learn from Jeremiah.

The book is structured in two broad parts as follows:

Jeremiah 1–25:	Destruction and loss
Jeremiah 26–52:	Restoration and hope

Naturally, each part has a complex presentation of texts and there is no need to see the whole book here. Part II is laid out as follows:

27:1–29:32	Differing theologies of hope
30:1–33:26	*The Book of Hope*

34:1–35:19	The new community
36:1–45:5	Hope amid disaster
46:1–51:64	Hope for the refugees
52:1–34	The restoration of King Jehoichin as a pledge of hope

Our Advent reading comes from the appropriately entitled *Book of Hope*.

Related passages

> Therefore a covenant of friendship was established with him, that he should be leader of the sanctuary and of his people, that he and his descendants should have the dignity of the priesthood forever. Just as a covenant was established with David son of Jesse of the tribe of Judah, that the king's heritage passes only from son to son, so the heritage of Aaron is for his descendants alone. (Sirach 45:24–25)

> The days are surely coming, says the Lord, when I will raise up for David a righteous Branch, and he shall reign as king and deal wisely, and shall execute justice and righteousness in the land. In his days Judah will be saved and Israel will live in safety. And this is the name by which he will be called: 'The LORD is our righteousness'. (Jeremiah 23:5–6)

Brief commentary

(V. 14)
The opening words in Hebrew are *Behold, the days are coming*. 'Says the Lord' is a weak translation of *'ne'um Adonai'* which might be better rendered 'I, the Lord, affirm'. The promise referred to is Jeremiah 23:5–6 (cited above).

(V.15)
The image of the Branch (sprig or twig) is part of a growing number of references to an ideal rule of the family of David, who would bring justice and peace in a way in which the recent Davidic rulers quite spectacularly failed. That was why the Lord cut down the tree of David

and only a stump was left. However, God will fulfil his eternal promise to David's line in 2 Samuel 7 by restoring Israel and raising up a future ruler. The key virtues sought in rulers are justice and righteousness.

(V. 16)

This is unimaginable during the Exile but promised nevertheless. 'Saved' is a good translation: for this nuance elsewhere see Psalm 119:117; Proverbs 28:18 (for the verb) and Psalm 12:6; Job 5:4, 11 (for the related noun). The name Joshua (in Greek, Jesus) comes from 'to save' and is referred to in Matthew: *She will give birth to a son and you will name him Jesus, because he will save his people from their sins.* (Matthew 1:21–22) 'The Lord is our righteousness' holds a negative assessment of the traditional monarchy and its failures. The last (failed) king of Judah was ironically named Zedekiah, a name that means 'my righteousness is Yahweh'.

Pointers for prayer

a) The passage from Jeremiah invites me to go back to times in my own life when God has shown himself to be faithful. Such personal experiences can be the ground of hope in later, perhaps more difficult, times. A prayer of hope.

b) In the 'righteous Branch for David' we, as Christians, see Jesus as the Messiah and Lord. Where do I see small signs of hope today in the community of faith? A prayer of discernment.

c) Where in my life do I find my security and safety? It might be good to name the people (especially) who provided support and nourishment, and also the times and places where support and nourishment came to me. A prayer of gratitude.

Prayer

God of our longing and God of all hope, in you we trust. When we are lost and do not know where to turn, your presence and your word sustain us.

Help us to be convinced that nothing can separate us from your love in Christ Jesus our Lord, your Son, who lives and reigns with you in the unity of the Holy Spirit, God for ever and ever. Amen.

Themes across the readings

The reading from Jeremiah is not apocalyptic and in that sense it does not prepare for the gospel. However, the gospel treats the second coming as a liberation, the completion of salvation; in that sense the first reading can be said to anticipate the third reading. Perhaps in particular the emphasis on integrity is echoed in the dire warning of Luke: *Watch yourselves, or your hearts will be coarsened with debauchery and drunkenness and the cares of life.*

Psalm 25 (24) is a prayer of trust and speaks of God's faithfulness, friendship and love. It should help us receive the first reading as people of faith.

Chapter 2

Advent 2C

Thought for the day

The feats of engineering hinted at in the citations from Isaiah may seem physically daunting, but they are even more of a challenge on the intended spiritual level. The highway is for our God – what in me impedes his way, how do I block the arrival of the Lord in my life? More positively, what do I do so that the Gospel may come alive in my life? With such cooperation from me, the Lord can and will bring to completion what he has begun.

Prayer

O God, you search me and you know me. Help me to know myself better; in particular, help me to acknowledge and set aside the blocks to your coming. You have indeed begun a good work in me and, in spite of my hesitations and resistance, I too want it to be brought to completion under your graceful care. Through Christ our Lord. Amen.

Gospel

Lk 3:1 In the fifteenth year of the reign of Emperor Tiberius, when Pontius Pilate was governor of Judea, and Herod was ruler of Galilee, and his brother Philip ruler of the region of Ituraea and Trachonitis, and Lysanias ruler of Abilene, [2] during the high priesthood of Annas and Caiaphas, the word of God came to John son of Zechariah in the wilderness. [3] He went into all the region around the Jordan, proclaiming a baptism of repentance for the forgiveness of sins, [4] as it is written in the book of the words of the prophet Isaiah, 'The voice of one crying out in the wilderness: "Prepare the way of the Lord, make his paths straight. ⁵ Every valley shall be filled, and every mountain and hill shall be made low, and the crooked shall be made straight, and the rough ways made smooth; ⁶ and all flesh shall see the salvation of God."'

Initial observations

John the Baptist is the quintessential Advent figure in the Christian tradition, preparing us even today for the arrival of Jesus. This gospel passage (together with next Sunday's) provides us with his basic teaching. The Isaiah citation marks John out as someone who prepares for someone else. John was immensely significant – to an uncomfortable degree it would seem – for early Christianity. (His followers, the Mandaeans, continue to exist today.)

Jesus had been a disciple of John and, as such, had accepted his baptism. Jesus' own ministry started from the moment his mentor could no longer function. Finally, Jesus' initial proclamation resembled that of John himself. In other words, John the Baptist was essential for the Jesus story and for that very reason each gospel is anxious to locate him as somehow preparatory or secondary. Mark's discovery and use of Isaiah 40 (followed by Matthew 3:3, Luke 3:4 and even John 1:23) was a stroke of genius.

Kind of writing

There is a literary introduction to the gospel in Luke 1:1–4. This is followed by the birth stories, Luke 1–2, laying foundations for the identity of Jesus. Finally, the actual story of the ministry of Jesus begins with this quite formal, second introduction. Later summaries in the Acts of the Apostles start with the ministry of John the Baptist.

The first verse sounds very much like the opening of an Old Testament book, linking John the Baptist with the prophetic tradition (Jeremiah 1:1; Hosea 1:1; Amos 1:1). Three different kinds of information are given here: (i) the setting in the wider political and religious world –

Luke 3:1–2a; (ii) the presentation of John as a prophet – Luke 3:2b–3; (iii) a proof text from the Hebrew Bible, locating John as a figure of fulfilment – Luke 3:4–6.

This rather grand opening echoes the style of Hellenistic biographies.

Old Testament background

> A voice cries out: 'In the wilderness prepare the way of the Lord, make straight in the desert a highway for our God. Every valley shall be lifted up, and every mountain and hill be made low; the uneven ground shall become level, and the rough places a plain. Then the glory of the Lord shall be revealed, and all people shall see it together, for the mouth of the Lord has spoken.' (Isaiah 40:3–5)

In using this quotation, Luke has made telling modifications to his source, Mark. He leaves out the citation from Malachi 3:1, relocating it to 7:27. He expands the citation to include Isaiah 40:4–5 in order to bring out the universal nature of the gospel. He omits the resemblance between John and Elijah, because, in this gospel, it is Jesus who is the Elijah-type figure. Finally, the reader will notice the difference in punctuation between the original Isaiah and the use in Luke (and Mark):

> A voice cries out: 'In the wilderness prepare the way of the Lord.' (Isaiah)

> The voice of one crying out in the wilderness: 'Prepare the way of the Lord.' (Luke)

It is not obviously practical to 'cry out in the wilderness' because no one will hear you!

Two other texts are cited or echoed in the last line of the citation:

> The Lord has bared his holy arm before the eyes of all the nations; and all the ends of the earth shall see the salvation of our God. (Isaiah 52:10)

'It shall be that whoever remains after all that I have foretold to you shall be saved and shall see my salvation and the end of my world.' (2 Esdras 6:25)

New Testament foreground

Disciples of John the Baptist continued right up to the end of the first century and beyond, as we can see from the Acts of the Apostles:

> He had been instructed in the Way of the Lord; and he spoke with burning enthusiasm and taught accurately the things concerning Jesus, though he knew only the baptism of John. (Acts 18:25)

> Then he said, 'Into what then were you baptised?' They answered, 'Into John's baptism.' Paul said, 'John baptised with the baptism of repentance, telling the people to believe in the one who was to come after him, that is, in Jesus.' (Acts 19:3–4)

St Paul

> For I am not ashamed of the gospel; it is the power of God for salvation to everyone who has faith, to the Jew first and also to the Greek. For in it the righteousness of God is revealed through faith for faith; as it is written, 'The one who is righteous will live by faith.' (Romans 1:16–17)

> For he says, 'At an acceptable time I have listened to you, and on a day of salvation I have helped you.' See, now is the acceptable time; see, now is the day of salvation! (2 Corinthians 6:2)

Brief commentary

(V.1)

Tiberius reigned from AD 14–37 and the fifteenth year would, in principle, be AD 28–29. This is the clearest dating of the ministry of John and therefore also of the ministry of Jesus, as far as it goes. Things are not quite as crisp as that because Tiberias had three years' co–regency before the death of Augustus and, in any case, different calendars were in use (Julian, Jewish, Syrian-Macedonian and Egyptian).

A complicating factor is the fact that the first three gospels portray a ministry of one year, while John's Gospel has a three-year ministry. John's time span is much more plausible. Pilate was prefect of Judea from AD 26–36.

Tetrarch meant a ruler of one fourth of a region, reflecting the division of the territory of Herod the Great, after his death. Herod Antipas ruled in Galilee (4 BC–AD 39) and his brother Philip was Tetrach of Ituraea and Trachonitis (4 BC–AD 34). Nothing whatsoever is known of Lysanias who ruled in Abilene, north of Galilee, in the anti-Lebanon mountain range. Why Luke would mention Lysanias *at all* is an enigma to scholars.

(V. 2)
Annas served as high priest from AD 6–15, and was succeeded by his son-in-law, Caiaphas, who served from AD 18–36. Technically, there was only one high priest at any one time, but people still regarded Annas as high priest, even if 'emeritus'.

Finally, the important expression is heard: 'The word of God came to X', is used with arresting frequency to introduce a man of God in the Old Testament (110 times in all, with Jeremiah as most representative – Jeremiah 1:2, 4, 11, 13; 2:1; 13:3, 8; 16:1; 18:5; 24:4; 28:12; 29:30; 32:6, 26; 33:1, 19, 23; 34:12; 35:12; 36:27; 37:6; 39:15; 42:7; 43:8). The evocation of Old Testament models is very effective. The wilderness is both literal and symbolic. As symbol, it recalls the place of Israel's formation as God's covenant people. The desert is the place of testing and the place of encounter.

(V. 3)
Four key terms are used: proclaiming, baptism, conversion (*metanoia*) and forgiveness. 'Proclaiming' means literally heralding (hence our word *kerygma*). The baptism of John was a prophetic gesture, involving a once-off immersion, to be distinguished from the later baptism of Christian tradition.

As usual, 'repentance' is not adequate here because it denotes only regret for the past, whereas *metanoia* points to a turning around, so as to get a radically new view and direction forward. In part, the turning around involves a change of behaviour, in response to forgiveness. *Metanoia* (as a verb) recurs only a few times in Luke: 3:8; 5:32; 15:7. However, it comes back resoundingly at the end of the gospel in Luke 24:45–47. There is a somewhat wider use in the Acts of the Apostles (Acts 5:31; 11:18; 13:24; 19:4; 20:21; 26:20).

(Vv. 4–5)
Luke has extended considerably the citation first found in Mark 1:2. By the adjustment of punctuation (noted above), the text is made to point to John the Baptist, who was the voice *crying out in the wilderness*.

(V. 6)
The last line is adjusted to 'all flesh shall see the salvation of God', echoing Isaiah 52:10 and 2 Esdras 6:25, as was seen above. In this way, Luke universalises even the ministry of John the Baptist, as a preparation for the proclamation of Jesus. Salvation (as noun and verb) does recur: Luke 1:47, 69, 71, 77; 2:11, 30; 3:6; 19:9; Acts 4:12; 5:31; 7:25; 13:23, 26, 47; 16:17; 27:34; 28:28. As a noun, the word saviour is not that common: Luke 1:47; 2:11; Acts 5:31; 13:23.

Pointers for prayer

a) The manner in which Luke identifies in detail the time when John the Baptist started his preaching shows that the evangelist regarded this as a historic moment. Perhaps you can recall in detail the time and the circumstances of particularly significant moments in your life?

b) John called people to give expression to their desire for a change of heart by a symbolic baptism in the Jordan. When have you found it helpful to symbolise your desire to change for the better by some symbolic gesture, for example burning a packet of cigarettes, sending a card or making a phone call?

c) Behind the quotation from Isaiah lies the practice of preparing festival routes for religious celebrations. Isaiah visualises such a celebration to celebrate the return of the Israelites to Jerusalem. Can you recall a particularly memorable Advent? What happened? Think of how you can do it this year.

Prayer

God of our salvation, you straighten the winding ways of our hearts and smooth the paths made rough by sin.

Make our conduct blameless, keep our hearts watchful in holiness, and bring to perfection the good you have begun in us.

We ask this through him whose coming is certain, whose day draws near: your Son, Jesus Christ, who lives and reigns with you in the unity of the Holy Spirit, God, for ever and ever. Amen.

Second Reading

Phil 1:3 *I thank my God every time I remember you.* ⁴ I always pray with joy in my every prayer for all of you ⁵ because of your participation in the gospel from the first day until now. ⁶ For I am sure of this very thing, that the one who began a good work in you will perfect it until the day of Christ Jesus. ⁷ *For it is right for me to think this about all of you, because I have you in my heart, since both in my imprisonment and in the defence and confirmation of the gospel all of you became partners in God's grace together with me.* ⁸ For God is my witness that I long for all of you with the affection of Christ Jesus. ⁹ And I pray this, that your love may abound even more and more in knowledge and every kind of insight ¹⁰ so that you can decide what is best, and thus be sincere and blameless for the day of Christ, ¹¹ filled with the fruit of righteousness that comes through Jesus Christ to the glory and praise of God.

Initial observations

Although this is not yet *Gaudete Sunday*, the readings already strike a note of joy. Philippians 1 takes up the joyful tone of the first reading, bringing it into our Christian perspective. The full thanksgiving is given above because Paul goes on to give concrete reasons for gratitude and joy. The appointed reading omits vv. 3 and 7, which are restored here.

Kind of writing

Philippians

Letter opening:	1:1–2
Introduction:	1:3–11
Situation:	1:12–26
Thesis:	1:27–30
Proof:	2:1–3:19
First development:	2:1–18
Second development:	2:19–3:1a
Third development:	3:1b–19
Conclusion:	3:20–4:20
Letter closing:	4:21–23

Our reading is part of the thanksgiving in a Pauline letter, itself an innovation of the apostle. Paul uses the thanksgiving to anticipate topics to come in the body of the letter (the so-called 'seeds of proof', or the *seminaprobationum*). He foreshadows, in a complimentary way, the problems to be tackled later in the letter.

Origin of the reading

Philippi was Paul's first community in Europe, established on the Second Missionary Journey. We know from 1 Thessalonians and 2 Corinthians how attached Paul remained to the Philippians and they to him.

The dating of the letter itself is disputed. Conceivably, it could have be written from Rome, Caesarea or Ephesus. Traditionally, the letter was written from Rome, just before Paul's own martyrdom. This would make Philippians his last letter and would document the apostle's state of mind right up to the end, perhaps c. AD 64. The chief evidence is reference to the *praetorium* (Philippians 1:13) and the household of Caesar (Philippians 4:22). However, such details could fit other cities as well. Caesarea is also mentioned as a possibility.

The letter seems to presuppose visits back and forth, which might be difficult with travel to distant Rome in mind (Philippians 2:19–30; 4:16–18). A more plausible proposal is Ephesus, about a week's distance from Philippi. This would imply a date somewhere in the mid-50s.

Related passages

We thank God always for all of you as we mention you constantly in our prayers, because we recall in the presence of our God and Father your work of faith and labour of love and endurance of hope in our Lord Jesus Christ. We know, brothers and sisters loved by God, that he has chosen you, in that our gospel did not come to you merely in words, but in power and in the Holy Spirit and with deep conviction (surely you recall the character we displayed when we came among you to help you). And you became imitators of us and of the Lord, when you received the message with joy that comes from the Holy Spirit, despite great affliction. As a result you became an example to all the believers in Macedonia and in Achaia. (1 Thessalonians 1:2–7)

First of all, I thank my God through Jesus Christ for all of you, because your faith is proclaimed throughout the whole world. For God, whom I serve in my spirit in the gospel of his Son, is my witness that I continually remember you and I always ask in my prayers, if perhaps now at last I may succeed in visiting you according to the will of God. For I long to see you, so that I may impart to you some spiritual gift to strengthen you, that is, that we may be mutually comforted by one another's faith, both yours and mine. (Romans 1:8–12)

I always thank my God as I remember you in my prayers, because I hear of your faith in the Lord Jesus and your love for all the saints. I pray that the faith you share with us may deepen your understanding of every blessing that belongs to you in Christ. I have had great joy and encouragement because of your love, for the hearts of the saints have been refreshed through you, brother. (Philemon 1:4–7)

Brief commentary

(V. 3)
Very typically, Paul's first prayer is one of thanksgiving for the communities he has founded. They form part of his relationship with God; when he thinks of them, his mind turns spontaneously to God and vice versa.

(V. 4)
Paul's prayer is constant ('always'; see the examples above) and joyful. In spite of all the stresses in his life and ministry, Paul is a happy believer and a joy-filled apostle.

(V. 5)
Two key words are used here. Participation translates *koinōnia*, which means participation, fellowship and communion (see Romans 15:26; 1 Corinthians 1:9; 10:16; 2 Corinthians 6:14; 8:4; 9:13; 13:13; Galatians 2:9; Philippians 1:5; 2:1; 3:10; Philemon 1:6). The Gospel, for Paul, means the proclamation of the death and resurrection of Jesus and the gift of the Holy Spirit. The word gospel is very common in Paul: see Philippians 1:5, 7, 12, 16, 27; 2:22; 4:3, 15, for example. 'From the first day' must mean from the start of the journeys of Paul.

(V. 6)
The first day suggests the last day, the Day of the Lord, towards which believers are journeying. Conversion is never 'over' but God is always at work on us. The language of the first day and the last day constitutes an echo of creation, when God began a work and also brought it to completion.

(V. 8)

Paul uses an oath formula to convey his sincere love for the Philippians. Compassion is especially rich. The word points to a deep inner attachment, almost physical, like the attachment of a mother to the child she bore.

(Vv. 9–10)

Paul prays explicitly and earnestly for the friends in Philippi. The prayer is both affirmative and forward-looking. As we remember those we love in prayer we could do worse than copy Paul's example here.

(V.11)

Harvest (fruit) is traditional 'end-time' language from the Bible. The topic of righteousness ('right relationship' with God) is central to Paul's thinking. It comes up in Galatians, Romans and Philippians – in all three place some were agitating for the full imposition of the ritual observances of Judaism. Paul's consistent position is that this is no longer necessary because Jesus' death and resurrection encompassed all humanity without distinction, as he puts it himself.

Pointers for prayer

a) For whom do I give thanks constantly? Who are the people who are part of my prayer? The words of Paul can help guide me here.

b) Teilhard de Chardin once said, 'There is something wonderful afoot in the universe!' And, we may add, in each one of us. God has begun a great work in me ... how do I see him bringing it to completion? How can I cooperate with the grace of God?

Prayer

Help me, loving God, to embrace your plans for me that what you have begun you may bring to completion. Through Christ our Lord. Amen.

🌿 First reading 🌿

Bar 5:1 Take off the garment of your sorrow and affliction,
O Jerusalem,
and put on forever the beauty of the glory from God.

2 Put on the robe of the righteousness that comes from God;
put on your head the diadem of the glory of the Everlasting;

3 for God will show your splendour everywhere under heaven.

4 For God will give you evermore the name,
'Righteous Peace, Godly Glory.'

5 Arise, O Jerusalem, stand upon the height;
look towards the east,
and see your children gathered from west and east
at the word of the Holy One,
rejoicing that God has remembered them.

6 For they went out from you on foot,
led away by their enemies;
but God will bring them back to you,
carried in glory, as on a royal throne.

7 For God has ordered that every high mountain
and the everlasting hills be made low
and the valleys filled up, to make level ground,
so that Israel may walk safely in the glory of God.

8 The woods and every fragrant tree
have shaded Israel at God's command.

9 For God will lead Israel with joy,
in the light of his glory,
with the mercy and righteousness that come from him.

Initial observations

This joy-filled poetic passage establishes the tone for Advent, a season of conversion marked by joy in believing. It would be easy not to feel joyful – but why take the easy way?

Kind of writing

Baruch 4:5–5:9 is a *prophetic address*, in which the prophet links the return from exile to conversion of heart. Although written so much later, the themes of Baruch are, nevertheless, exile, disobedience, conversion and return. This reminded people that the current oppression would also come to an end, as had previous ones.

Origin of the reading

Baruch is one of the Deuterocanonical books. This reflects the fact that while a Hebrew original is conceivable, the earliest extant text of Baruch is in Greek. Broadly speaking, the consensus is that Baruch was written during the 'Greek' period, 332–63 BC, most likely in the second century BC. Rather more precisely, there is a hypothesis that it was written at a time when a portion of the Jewish population in Jerusalem had come to an 'understanding' with their overlords, the Seleucids, and were urging fellow Jews to do likewise. Such considerations lead scholars to posit 163–162 as the time of writing.

Related passages

For a change, the related passages are linked to each verse in Baruch.

Vv. 1–2 Awake, awake, put on your strength, O Zion! Put on your beautiful garments, O Jerusalem, the holy city; for the uncircumcised and the unclean shall enter you no more. (Isaiah 52:1; cf. 61:10)

V. 4 The nations shall see your vindication, and all the kings your glory; and you shall be called by a new name that the mouth of the LORD will give. You shall be a crown of beauty in the hand of the LORD, and a royal diadem in the hand of your God. You shall no more be termed Forsaken, and your land shall no more be termed Desolate; but you shall be called My Delight Is in Her, and your land Married; for the LORD delights in you, and your land shall be married. (Isaiah 62:2–4)

V. 5 Get you up to a high mountain, O Zion, herald of good tidings; lift up your voice with strength, O Jerusalem, herald of good tidings, lift it up, do not fear; say to the cities of Judah, 'Here is your God!' (Isaiah 40:9; cf. 43:4–7; 51:17; 60:4)

V. 6 Thus says the Lord GOD: I will soon lift up my hand to the nations, and raise my signal to the peoples; and they shall bring your sons in their bosom, and your daughters shall be carried on their shoulders. (Isaiah 49:22)

V. 7 Every valley shall be lifted up, and every mountain and hill be made low; the uneven ground shall become level, and the rough places a plain. Then the glory of the LORD shall be revealed, and all people shall see it together, for the mouth of the LORD has spoken.' (Isaiah 40:4–5)

V. 9 Arise, shine; for your light has come, and the glory of the LORD has risen upon you. For darkness shall cover the earth, and thick darkness the peoples; but the LORD will arise upon you, and his glory will appear over you. Nations shall come to your light, and kings to the brightness of your dawn. (Isaiah 60:1–3)

Brief commentary

(V. 1)
The first verse sounds the only 'negative' note and the rest of the reading is immensely positive. V.1a is matched by v. 1b in antithetical parallelism. The beauty 'from God' is expanded and explored in the following verses.

(V. 2)
Again, two lines in parallel: a covering for the body and crown for the head. The robe, however, is the 'robe of righteousness'. The gift of right relationship with God will be evident externally ('robe') by how we live.

(V. 3)
A universal promise of salvation, indicated by 'under heaven'.

(V. 4)

A new name means a new identity *and reality*. The affirmations here are extraordinary. Peace – shalom – is God's gift of wholeness and wellness. Glory, in Hebrew, points not to external brilliance but to the inner reality of God's being. The vision invites both awe and gratitude.

(V. 5)

Jerusalem is addressed and invited to look east – even though her children come from east and west. The cause of this gathering of the dispersed is 'God has remembered them'. This 'remembering' of God is the foundation of Israelite memorial or *zikkron*. Cf. For he remembered his holy promise, and Abraham, his servant. (Psalm 105:42)

(V. 6)

A happy contrast is drawn between the abject conditions of deportation and the majestic return.

(V. 7)

God is portrayed as a 'civil engineer', levelling the roads. Cf. Isaiah 40. God is making it easy for them to undertake the journey of the heart.

(V. 8)

Even nature joins in and does its bit for those on the way home. The feeling of coolness would be very welcome in the Middle East.

(V. 9)

The ground for all this hope is God's mercy and righteousness, his covenant qualities from of old. Notice that the joy mentioned is attributed to God in the first place.

Pointers for prayer

a) It is easy to give in to the temptation of downheartedness. Can you hear the call to a more joyful, life-giving experience of the faith?

b) The reading calls us to go back into our own experience. When have you known such grace in the past and does the memory of that reality sustain you today?

Prayer

God, Holy One, everlasting and full of mercy, in you we place all our trust. In times of distress, open our hearts to true life and joy in believing that we have new courage and be sources of encouragement to all we meet. Through Christ our Lord. Amen.

Themes across the readings

The first reading, which picks up the language of Second Isaiah, prepares us for the citation from Isaiah in relation to the ministry of John the Baptist. Mark was the first to use this citation and Luke, in his redaction, expands and enriches it. Although Baruch was written much later than the actual exile in Babylon, Psalm 126 from the time of the deportation itself captures the joy of such liberation, past and future.

Chapter 3

Advent 3C

Thought for the day

'What then should we do?' is both obvious and pertinent. In the maelstrom of life, it is good to stand back and discern what is being asked of me in the many contexts of life: family member, spouse, parent, disciple, leader, pastor, evangeliser and so forth. In these different roles, how should I be, what should I do so as to enable others too to fulfil their own callings, as family member, spouse etc. As in the teaching of John the Baptist, our responses are authentic only if they are practical, down-to-earth and real.

Prayer

Help me, Lord, to recognise in the everyday what you desire of me. Help me to see what are the practical steps I can take from today onwards so as to be a better disciple of your son, Jesus, the coming one, whom John proclaims today to all who would listen. Through the same Christ our Lord. Amen.

Gospel

Lk 3:10 And the crowds asked John, 'What then should we do?' [11] In reply he said to them, 'Whoever has two coats must share with anyone who has none; and whoever has food must do likewise.' [12] Even tax collectors came to be baptised, and they asked him, 'Teacher, what should we do?' [13] He said to them, 'Collect no more than the amount prescribed for you.' [14] Soldiers also asked him, 'And we, what should we do?' He said to them, 'Do not extort money from anyone by threats or false accusation, and be satisfied with your wages.'

[15] As the people were filled with expectation, and all were questioning in their hearts concerning John, whether he might be the Messiah, [16] John answered all of them by saying, 'I baptise you with water; but one who is more powerful than I is coming; I am not worthy to untie the thong of his sandals. He will baptise you with the Holy Spirit and fire. [17] His winnowing fork is in his hand, to clear his threshing floor and to gather the wheat into his granary; but the chaff he will burn with unquenchable fire.'

[18] So, with many other exhortations, he proclaimed the good news to the people.

Initial observations

Luke gives a more extended summary of the preaching of the Baptist, a measure of his continued significance (see New Testament foreground below). Cf. Luke 3:1–9.

In Luke, the birth narratives of John and Jesus are designed to 'sort' the relationship between the two. However, continued anxiety is apparent in Luke's extraordinary editorial move in removing the Baptist from the scene of the baptism: *But Herod the ruler, who had been rebuked by him because of Herodias, his brother's wife, and because of all the evil things that Herod had done, added to them all by shutting up John in prison. Now when all the people were baptised, and when Jesus also had been baptised and was praying, the heaven was opened, and the Holy Spirit descended upon him in bodily form like a dove. And a voice came from heaven, 'You are my Son, the Beloved; with you I am well pleased'* (Luke 3:19–22).

Kind of writing

It is a summary statement of John's preaching, confirmed in Josephus' account. The clear distinction between John and Jesus was needed both at the time of writing and later.

Old Testament background

What should we do?

These are the things that you shall do: Speak the truth to one another, render in your gates judgments that are true and make for peace, do not devise evil in your hearts against one another, and love no false oath; for all these are things that I hate, says the Lord. (Zechariah 8:16–17)

Baptism of Fire

On that day the branch of the Lord shall be beautiful and glorious, and the fruit of the land shall be the pride and glory of the survivors of Israel. Whoever is left in Zion and remains in Jerusalem will be called holy, everyone who has been recorded for life in Jerusalem, once the Lord has washed away the filth of the daughters of Zion and cleansed the bloodstains of Jerusalem from its midst by a spirit of judgment and by a spirit of burning. Then the Lord will create over the whole site of Mount Zion and over its places of assembly a cloud by day and smoke and the shining of a flaming fire by night. Indeed over all the glory there will be a canopy. (Isaiah 4:2–5)

See, the day is coming, burning like an oven, when all the arrogant and all evildoers will be stubble; the day that comes shall burn them up, says the Lord of hosts, so that it will leave them neither root nor branch. (Malachi 4:1)

Harvest symbolism

They are like trees planted by streams of water, which yield their fruit in its season, and their leaves do not wither. In all that they do, they prosper. The wicked are not so, but are like chaff that the wind drives away. (Psalm 1:3–4)

I have winnowed them with a winnowing fork in the gates of the land; I have bereaved them, I have destroyed my people; they did not turn from their ways. (Jeremiah 15:7)

Expectations (extra-biblical)

And he will be a righteous king over them, taught by God. There will be no unrighteousness among them in his days, for all shall be holy, and their king shall be the Lord Messiah. (Psalms of Solomon 17:32)

May God cleanse Israel for the day of mercy in blessing, for the appointed day when his Messiah will reign. (which will be) under the rod of discipline of the Lord Messiah, in the fear of his God, in wisdom of spirit, and of righteousness and of strength.' (Psalms of Solomon 18:5, 7)

Good news – an expression from Second and Third Isaiah

Get you up to a high mountain, O Zion, herald of good tidings; lift up your voice with strength, O Jerusalem, herald of good tidings, lift it up, do not fear; say to the cities of Judah, 'Here is your God!' (Isaiah 40:9; cf. Isaiah 52:7)

The spirit of the Lord GOD is upon me, because the LORD has anointed me; he has sent me to bring good news to the oppressed, to bind up the brokenhearted, to proclaim liberty to the captives, and release to the prisoners; to proclaim the year of the Lord's favour (Isaiah 61:1–2)

New Testament foreground

He answered them, 'I will also ask you a question, and you tell me: Did the baptism of John come from heaven, or was it of human origin?' They discussed it with one another, saying, 'If we say, "From heaven," he will say, "Why did you not believe him?" But if we say, "Of human origin," all the people will stone us; for they are convinced that John was a prophet.' (Luke 20:3–6)

He had been instructed in the Way of the Lord; and he spoke with burning enthusiasm and taught accurately the things concerning Jesus, though he knew only the baptism of John. (Acts 18:25)

Then he said, 'Into what then were you baptised?' They
answered, 'Into John's baptism.' Paul said, 'John baptised with
the baptism of repentance, telling the people to believe in
the one who was to come after him, that is, in Jesus.' (Acts
19:3–4)

St Paul

Owe no one anything, except to love one another; for the one
who loves another has fulfilled the law. The commandments,
'You shall not commit adultery; You shall not murder;
You shall not steal; You shall not covet'; and any other
commandment, are summed up in this word, 'Love your
neighbour as yourself.' Love does no wrong to a neighbour;
therefore, love is the fulfilling of the law. (Romans 13:8–10)

Brief commentary

(V.10)
These questions are in Luke only and the message is addressed to the
crowds, that is the people, as such, and not just to their leaders. A life of
practical conversion of heart, leading to real service of the neighbour is
what John has in mind.

(V. 11)
Looking out for the poor is part of Old Testament piety: Isaiah 1:10–
20; 58:6–7 and many other texts. At Luke's stage in the evolution of
Christianity, disciples looked forward urgently to a reversal of oppressive
social conditions.

(V. 12)
As is well known, tax collectors were mostly likely fellow Jews who
worked for the empire. They were regarded as traitors and were well
known for corrupt practices.

(V.13)
This verse acknowledges the corrupt practices of the tax/toll collectors.

(V. 14)

Soldiers, too, could have included Jews, in the service of Herod Antipas. This teaching of John is confirmed in the writings of Josephus, the Jewish historian of the period.

(V. 15)

Some clearly did regard John as the Messiah. He himself seems to have been clear that he was not. However, what he *did* expect is not so clear: God himself perhaps, or an angel, or the Messiah or a Moses-type prophet.

(V. 16)

John distinguishes himself from the Messiah in three ways. (i) The messiah will be someone 'more powerful.' (ii) John uses as a metaphor the humblest task of the lowest servant. (iii) There will be a different kind of baptism. It may well be that originally the image was simpler: wind (*pneuma*, also spirit) and fire, that is, elements associated with harvest (see the next verse). The Christian reception of the image, however, reads *pneuma* to mean Spirit, to which the label 'holy' is given so that it now refers to the Holy Spirit in baptism. In turn, then, the Holy Spirit has a large presence and role in Luke–Acts (Luke 1:15, 35, 41, 67; 2:25–26; 3:16, 22; 4:1; 10:21; 11:13; 12:10, 12; Acts 1:2, 5, 8, 16; 2:4, 33, 38; 4:8, 25, 31; 5:3, 32; 6:5; 7:51 and so forth).

(V. 17)

This is the traditional image of harvest for the end of time. When harvest does come around, it is time to examine the quality of the crop and so it easily becomes a metaphor of judgement, for instance in Psalm 1 above. The image comes from farming practice: the whole mixture was thrown into the air and the wind blew the chaff aside, while the grain landed. The chaff was then burned. Of course, the fire at a harvest was not unquenchable. This points us in the direction of final judgement.

Cf. And they shall go out and look at the dead bodies of the people who have rebelled against me; for their worm shall not die, their fire shall not be quenched, and they shall be an abhorrence to all flesh. (Isaiah 66:24)

Pointers for prayer

a) What should we do?'The common thread in John's answers was to encourage his questioners to be other-centred rather than self-centred, each in the context of their own circumstances. In your experience what difference has it made for you when you changed your attitude in this way?

b) John told the people in a direct and honest way what they should do. Perhaps you have had friends who did not beat about the bush but have told you honestly what they thought about your behaviour when you asked them. In gratitude recall such friends.

c) The humility of John comes out in this passage, happy to acknowledge that he had only a minor role to play in relation to the Messiah. At the same time he was enthused by his mission to 'proclaim the good news to the people'. What difference has it made for you when you were able to see the good in yourself, and use your gifts without having to score by portraying yourself as greater than someone else?

Prayer

Almighty God, you sent your Son into a world where the wheat must be winnowed from the chaff and evil clings even to what is good. Let the fire of your Spirit purge us of greed and deceit, so that, purified, we may find our peace in you and you may delight in us.

Grant this through him whose coming is certain, Jesus Christ, who lives and reigns with you in the unity of the Holy Spirit, God, for ever and ever. Amen.

🌿 Second reading 🌿

Phil 4:4 Rejoice in the Lord always; again I will say, Rejoice. [5] Let your gentleness be known to everyone. The Lord is near. [6] Do not worry about anything, but in everything by prayer and supplication with thanksgiving let your requests be made known to God. [7] And the peace of God, which surpasses all understanding, will guard your hearts and your minds in Christ Jesus.

Initial observations

Faith today can be rather anguished. It may very well be that the word we need is 'rejoice'. It is easy to fall victim to the conventional view and deny ourselves access to real happiness in believing. Paul was a happy man. His word of joy is the very thing we find hardest and yet most need.

Kind of writing

Our passage comes from the conclusion in the letter, where Paul is exhorting them to happiness in believing.

Philippians
Letter opening:	1:1–2
Introduction:	1:3–11
Situation:	1:12–26
Thesis:	1:27–30
Proof:	2:1–3:19
First development:	2:1–18
Second development:	2:19–3:1a
Third development:	3:1b–19
Conclusion:	3:20–4:20
Letter closing:	4:21–23

Paul often concludes his teaching with a kind of 'spitfire' or staccato exhortation, as here. Another good illustration would be 1 Thessalonians 5:16–22 (see below).

Origin of the reading

For introductory observations on the context in Philippi, see last week's notes.

At this stage, Paul was under arrest. The Philippians learned of his imprisonment and they sent Epaphroditus with a gift to deliver to Paul. Epaphroditus fell seriously ill on his way to Paul and nearly died. The Philippians learned of Epaphroditus's illness and became concerned. Epaphroditus recovered, completed his journey to Paul, and delivered the gift. Epaphroditus then learned of the Philippians' anxiety for him and he, in his turn, became distressed on account of them. Paul sent Epaphroditus back to Philippi with a letter in which he commended Epaphroditus, thanked the Philippians for their gift, warned them about false teachers, and informed them about his own circumstances and plans.

Related passages

> For how can we thank God enough for you, for all the joy we feel because of you before our God? (1 Thessalonians 3:9)

> Always rejoice, constantly pray, in everything give thanks. For this is God's will for you in Christ Jesus. Do not extinguish the Spirit. Do not treat prophecies with contempt. But examine all things; hold fast to what is good. Stay away from every form of evil. (1 Thessalonians 5:16–22)

> What is the result? Only that in every way, whether in pretence or in truth, Christ is being proclaimed, and in this I rejoice. Yes, and I will continue to rejoice, for I know that this will turn out for my deliverance through your prayers and the help of the Spirit of Jesus Christ. (Philippians 1:18–19)

> But even if I am being poured out like a drink offering on the sacrifice and service of your faith, I am glad and rejoice together with all of you. And in the same way you also should be glad and rejoice together with me. (Philippians 2:17–18)

Finally, my brothers and sisters, rejoice in the Lord! (Philippians 3:1)

But the fruit of the Spirit is love, joy, peace, patience, kindness, goodness, faithfulness, gentleness, and self-control. Against such things there is no law. (Galatians 5:22–23)

Rejoice in hope, endure in suffering, persist in prayer. Contribute to the needs of the saints, pursue hospitality. Bless those who persecute you, bless and do not curse. Rejoice with those who rejoice, weep with those who weep. (Romans 12:12–15)

And what you learned and received and heard and saw in me, do these things. And the God of peace will be with you. (Philippians 4:9)

Brief commentary

(V. 4)
The rejoicing is to be done 'in the Lord', that is, as part of our believing and not mere natural effervescence.

(V. 5)
The translation 'gentleness' for *epieikēs* is perhaps a little weak. The Jerusalem Bible in the lectionary has 'tolerance', but it is rather more proactive than tolerance and more robust than gentleness. Other uses of both *epieikēs* and *epieikeia* with related synonyms in the New Testament may help: But, to detain you no further, I beg you to hear us briefly with your *customary graciousness* (Acts 24:4). I myself, Paul, appeal to you by the *meekness* and *gentleness* of Christ (2 Corinthians 10:1). But the wisdom from above is first pure, then peaceable, *gentle, willing to yield*, full of mercy and good fruits, without a trace of partiality or hypocrisy (James 3:17). Slaves, accept the authority of your masters with all deference, not only those who are *kind* and *gentle* but also those who are harsh (1 Peter 2:18). The New English Bible has *magnanimity*, which is quite good.

The sudden affirmation that the Lord is near seems to stem from the previous 'always' and leads to the next verse. Cf. *But our citizenship is in heaven, and it is from there that we are expecting a Saviour, the Lord Jesus Christ* (Philippians 3:20).

(V. 6)
Paul resembles here the teaching in Matthew 6:25–34 (or is it the other way around?). Thanksgiving is always very much part of Paul's prayer, even when interceding.

(V. 7)
Peace, in this context, is again very proactive and robust. It takes us well beyond absence of conflict to total well-being and a life-attitude that comes from Christ himself. Of the many references to peace in Paul's letters, perhaps one will suffice to illustrate: *To set the mind on the flesh is death, but to set the mind on the Spirit is life and peace* (Romans 8:6; cf. Romans 1:7; 2:10; 3:17; 5:1; 8:6; 14:17, 19; 15:13, 33; 16:20; 1 Corinthians 1:3; 7:15; 14:33; 16:11; 2 Corinthians 1:2; 13:11; Galatians 1:3; 5:22; 6:16; Philippians 1:2; 4:7, 9; 1 Thessalonians 1:1; 5:3, 23; Philemon 1:3).

Pointers for prayer

a) Is joy really part of my believing? Would anyone be able to tell?

b) Where in my own life do I need that peace that comes from God alone?

c) For what should I now give thanks? Is being thankful part of who I am?

Prayer

Loving God, you read our hearts and know us better than we know ourselves. Open our hearts to the peace that you alone can give. Let us have that joy in believing that will strengthen our faith in you and confirm our witness to you, the source of all that is good. Through Christ our Lord. Amen.

🍃 First reading 🍃

Zeph 3:14   Sing aloud, O daughter Zion;
       shout, O Israel!
   Rejoice and exult with all your heart,
       O daughter Jerusalem!
¹⁵   The Lord has taken away the judgments against you,
       he has turned away your enemies.
   The king of Israel, the Lord, is in your midst;
       you shall fear disaster no more.
¹⁶   On that day it shall be said to Jerusalem:
   Do not fear, O Zion;
       do not let your hands grow weak.
¹⁷   The Lord, your God, is in your midst,
       a warrior who gives victory;
   he will rejoice over you with gladness,
       he will renew you in his love;
   he will exult over you with loud singing
¹⁸   as on a day of festival.
   I will remove disaster from you,
       so that you will not bear reproach for it.

Initial observations

The short Book of Zephaniah (only three chapters) was written at a very interesting time. This otherwise unknown prophet worked in Jerusalem when Josiah was king (640–609 BC). The northern kingdom was already under Assyrian rule and the southern kingdom was about to fall under their control. Even so, the ruling classes in Jerusalem, including the priests, had compromised ahead of time with Assyrian culture and religion. Zephaniah excoriates this accommodation with its inevitable idolatry and syncretism. His great theme is the Day of the Lord, a day of calamity and judgement, which will lead to a purified remnant. Parts seem to be post-exilic, as we shall see.

Kind of writing

The speeches of Zephaniah are highly rhetorical, aimed at the 'humble in the land' and designed to evoke from them a response. By seeking God, the humble may escape the coming judgement and be spared so as to enjoy the purified Jerusalem. Faith and hope will eventually lead to joy. It assumes Zephaniah 3:8–13 has already taken place.

The writing is poetry. It achieves its effects by (i) parallelism; (ii) repetition of key phrases; (iii) the emotional contrast with the preceding material.

Origin of the reading

The book has the following straightforward structure:

(1:1)	Title
(1:2–6)	Judgement
(1:7–18)	Exhortation to silence
(2:1–3:7)	Exhortation to seek YHWH
(3:8–13)	Exhortation to wait
(3:14–20)	Exhortation to rejoice

The book starts with a judgement over all creation (1:2–6, a *tour de force* which reverses Genesis) and closes with a celebration in a restored Jerusalem, where the exiles have returned as a remnant (3:14–12). Our reading, therefore, is the very last section of the book (the remaining verses have been added here for the sake of completeness).

Related passages

> Sing and rejoice, O daughter Zion! For lo, I will come and dwell in your midst, says the Lord. (Zechariah 2:10)

> Rejoice greatly, O daughter Zion! Shout aloud, O daughter Jerusalem! Lo, your king comes to you; triumphant and victorious is he, humble and riding on a donkey, on a colt, the foal of a donkey. (Zechariah 9:9)

Do not fear, for you will not be ashamed; do not be discouraged, for you will not suffer disgrace; for you will forget the shame of your youth, and the disgrace of your widowhood you will remember no more. (Isaiah 54:4)

For as a young man marries a young woman, so shall your builder marry you, and as the bridegroom rejoices over the bride, so shall your God rejoice over you. (Isaiah 62:5)

I will restore the fortunes of my people Israel, and they shall rebuild the ruined cities and inhabit them; they shall plant vineyards and drink their wine, and they shall make gardens and eat their fruit. I will plant them upon their land, and they shall never again be plucked up out of the land that I have given them, says the LORD your God. (Amos 9:14–15)

Brief commentary

(V. 14)
The verse proclaims a public celebration of the return and purification. The community in Jerusalem is addressed. The grounds for such uninhibited rejoicing are given in the next verse: God's presence.

(V. 15)
The punishment has been reversed. Notice that now the Lord is king. In the midst: cf. *God is in the midst of the city; it shall not be moved; God will help it when the morning dawns* (Psalm 46:5).

(V.16)
The day is no longer the day of judgement but the day of liberation. 'Do not be afraid' is said to very many people in the Bible (e.g. Genesis 15:1; 21:17; 26:24; 35:17; 43:23; 46:3; 50:19; Exodus 14:13; 20:20, taking illustrations just from Genesis and Exodus).

(Vv. 17–18a)
'The Lord is in your midst' is repeated from v. 15. Hence the profound feeling of security. The martial imagery yields to nuptial language (see Isaiah 62:5 above), that is, God protects because of his love. Notice that

God is said to shout, in response to Israel's shout of joy. It may, of course, seem appealing that the Lord should dance, but not all translators agree.

(V. 18bc)
This extremely difficult verse in Hebrew (not in the excerpt to be read) is resolved rather breezily in the original Jerusalem Bible. In any case here are some alternatives:*'As for those who grieve because they cannot attend the festivals– I took them away from you; they became tribute and were a source of shame to you'* (Zephaniah 3:18, New English Translation); *He will soothe with his love those long disconsolate. I will take away from you the woe over which you endured mockery* (Zephaniah 3:17–18, Jewish Publication Society translations).*He will dance with shouts of joy for you, on a day of festival. I have taken away your misfortune, no longer need you bear the disgrace of it* (Zephaniah 3:17–18, Revised New Jerusalem Bible).

Pointers for prayer

a) When have I felt happiness in believing, real joy on account of the faith?

b) Do not be afraid: these days do we resist easy reassurance even in faith (opium)?

Prayer

God of all joy, you delight in each one of us and we thank you from our hearts for your great love. May the joy of believing in you help us to be bearers of your truly Good News in our world today. Through Christ our Lord. Amen.

Themes across the readings

Given the special arrangements for the Advent readings, the link between Zephaniah and Luke is not so clear. However, the joy proclaimed by the prophet captures the mood of anticipation, on the cusp of the arrival of God's Messiah. The responsorial psalm is a canticle from Isaiah 12 and picks up perfectly the tone of unrestrained joy. *Gaudete* is the unmistakable message.

Chapter 4

Advent 4C

Thought for the day

Even in its resolutely secular form, the Christmas celebration has positive sides to it. People do try very hard to get together with close family and friends. It might help to reflect *in advance* on this seasonal intensity of encounter. What do I hope for? What do I bring? How can I/we be so that we are not simply in the same physical space but truly meet each other and are the better for it? There should be some leap of joy, so that, at the end of the festivities, we are glad we made the effort.

Prayer

God of all loving, bless all our encounters this Christmas. Help us to be both kind and joyful, so that all whom we meet will be the better for it. Inspire us to know when a word of witness will lift the celebration and enable family and friends to get to the heart of it all. Through Christ our Lord. Amen.

Gospel

Lk 1:39 In those days Mary set out and went with haste to a Judean town in the hill country, [40] where she entered the house of Zechariah and greeted Elizabeth. [41] When Elizabeth heard Mary's greeting, the child leaped in her womb.

And Elizabeth was filled with the Holy Spirit [42] and exclaimed with a loud cry, 'Blessed are you among women, and blessed is the fruit of your womb. [43] And why has this happened to me, that the mother of my Lord comes to me? [44] For as soon as I heard the sound of your greeting, the child in my womb leaped for joy. [45] And blessed is she who believed that there would be a fulfilment of what was spoken to her by the Lord.'

[46] *And Mary said, 'My soul magnifies the Lord,* [47] *and my spirit rejoices in God my Saviour,* [48] *for he has looked with favour on the lowliness of his servant. Surely, from now on all generations will call me blessed;* [49] *for the Mighty One has done great things for me, and holy is his name.*

[50] *His mercy is for those who fear him from generation to generation.* [51] *He has shown strength with his arm; he has scattered the proud in the thoughts of their hearts.* [52] *He has brought down the powerful from their thrones, and lifted up the lowly;* [53] *he has filled the hungry with good things, and sent the rich away empty.* [54] *He has helped his servant Israel, in remembrance of his mercy,* [55] *according to the promise he made to our ancestors, to Abraham and to his descendants forever.'*

[56] *And Mary remained with her about three months and then returned to her home.*

Initial observations

The lectionary offers the short form of the story, but the Magnificat is equally part of it and is therefore restored here. This vignette, unique to Luke, brings the two prophets together in their respective mothers' wombs. As such, it forms part of Luke's theology that John and Jesus are related, on the level of the history of salvation, and, at the same time, that the second prophet, Jesus, is greater than the first, John. This distinction is already made clear in the various things that have been said about each child (see the annunciations to Zechariah and to Mary), and now, John, an unconscious child, signals the arrival of the Messiah. The passage that follows this greeting by Elizabeth is one of the most subversive in the New Testament, Mary's hymn of praise, the Magnificat.

How historical these stories might be can be gauged from a story later in Luke's Gospel:

The disciples of John reported all these things to him. So John summoned two of his disciples and sent them to the Lord to ask, 'Are you the one who is to come, or are we to wait for another?' When the men had come to him, they said, 'John the Baptist has sent us to you to ask, 'Are you the one who is to come, or are we to wait for another?'' Jesus had just then cured many people of diseases, plagues, and evil spirits, and had given sight to many who were blind. And he answered them, 'Go and tell John what you have seen and heard: the blind receive their sight, the lame walk, the lepers are cleansed, the deaf hear, the dead are raised, the poor have good news brought to them. And blessed is anyone who takes no offence at me.' (Luke 7:18–23)

And Mary remained with her about three months and then returned to her home (Luke 1:56). That Mary stays three months and then departs is arresting (six and three being nine), but the presence of Mary at the birth of John would have complicated the narrative unnecessarily and would have served no purpose.

Kind of writing

This single scene makes sense only against the background of Luke 1–2 (or even Luke 1:5–4:15) as a whole. The Infancy Narrative of Luke may be seen to fall into seven very skilfully constructed tableaux, as in the table below. Each scene has three characteristics as described below.

1. *Annunciation* of the birth of John: 1:5–25	2. *Annunciation* of the birth of Jesus: 1:26–38
3. The *Visitation*: John 'acknowledges' Jesus: 1:39–56	
4. The *Birth* of John: 1:57–80	5. The *Birth* of Jesus: 2:1–21
6. The *Presentation* in the Temple: 2:22–40	
7. The boy Jesus *teaches* in the Temple: 2:41–52	

(1) Each tableau begins with a setting of the *scene*, whether historical or biblical. (2) Entry of chief *personality/personalities*, and in due course, their exit/a concluding statement. (3) Climax in the form of some kind of *revelation* (which highlights the theological significance of the scene of the angel's message in 1, 2 and 5; an inspired canticle in 3, 4 and 6 and Jesus' first recorded words in 7).

The only 'encounter' between the two sets of protagonists in Luke 1–2 is the Visitation, which thereby has an almost disproportionate significance.

Old Testament background

> Blessed shall be the fruit of your womb, the fruit of your ground, and the fruit of your livestock, both the increase of your cattle and the issue of your flock. (Deuteronomy 28:4)

> Then Uzziah said to her, 'O daughter, you are blessed by the Most High God above all other women on earth; and blessed be the Lord GOD, who created the heavens and the earth, who has guided you to cut off the head of the leader of our enemies. Your praise will never depart from the hearts of those who remember the power of God. May God grant this to be a perpetual honour to you, and may he reward you with blessings, because you risked your own life when our nation was brought low, and you averted our ruin, walking in the straight path before our God.' And all the people said, 'Amen. Amen'. (Judith 13:18–20 – not *wholly* inappropriate given the political nature of the Magnificat!)

New Testament foreground

There are explicit connections with the rest of the gospel. These links are always on a thematic level; no one within the ministry ever seems to 'remember' any of this, not even John the Baptist himself. But the theological themes anticipated here are present in the two volumes of Luke–Acts. The abundance of citations makes the point.

'To fill' or 'to fulfil': Luke 1:15, 20, 23, 41, 57, 67; 2:6, 21–22, 40; 3:5; 4:21, 28; 5:7, 26; 6:11; 7:1; 9:31; 21:22, 24; 22:16; 24:44; Acts 1:16; 2:2, 4, 28; 3:10, 18; 4:8, 31; 5:3, 17, 28; 7:23, 30; 9:17, 23; 12:25; 13:9, 25, 27, 45, 52; 14:26; 19:21, 29; 24:27.

Holy Spirit: Luke 1:15, 35, 41, 67; 2:25–26; 3:16, 22; 4:1; 10:21; 11:13; 12:10, 12; Acts 1:2, 5, 8, 16; 2:4, 33, 38; 4:8, 25, 31; 5:3, 32; 6:5; 7:51, 55; 8:15, 17, 19; 9:17, 31; 10:38, 44–45, 47; 11:15–16, 24; 13:2, 4, 9, 52; 15:8, 28; 16:6; 19:2, 6; 20:23, 28; 21:11; 28:25.

Joy, rejoice: Luke 1:14, 44, 47; 10:21.

Blessed: Luke 1:45; 6:20–22; 7:23; 10:23; 11:27–28; 12:37–38, 43; 14:14–15; 23:29.

> At that same hour Jesus rejoiced in the Holy Spirit and said, 'I thank you, Father, Lord of heaven and earth, because you have hidden these things from the wise and the intelligent and have revealed them to infants; yes, Father, for such was your gracious will. All things have been handed over to me by my Father; and no one knows who the Son is except the Father, or who the Father is except the Son and anyone to whom the Son chooses to reveal him.' (Luke 10:21–22)

St Paul

> But even if I am being poured out as a libation over the sacrifice and the offering of your faith, I am glad and rejoice with all of you – and in the same way you also must be glad and rejoice with me. (Philippians 2:17–18)

> Finally, my brothers and sisters, rejoice in the Lord. (Philippians 3:1)

> Rejoice in the Lord always; again I will say, Rejoice. (Philippians 4:4)

> I rejoice in the Lord greatly that now at last you have revived your concern for me; indeed, you were concerned for me, but had no opportunity to show it. (Philippians 4:10)

Brief commentary

The two storylines of birth are brought together here. Elizabeth pronounces a brief exclamation of praise and Mary a much longer canticle.

(V.39)
The 'hill country' and 'Judah' are mentioned again in Luke 1:65. Tradition has identified the town as Ein Kerem (in southwest Jerusalem today).

(V. 40)
Mentioning Zechariah reminds us of the earlier annunciation to him, which opened Luke's narrative and called to mind the pattern of annunciation stories.

(V. 41)
The leaping – the 'quickening' of the womb – is symbolic of the arrival of salvation. For Luke's purposes, it constitutes an acknowledgement of the Messiah by the Baptist. As above, the Holy Spirit is the energy behind the Jesus project and the proclamation of the Good News. For leaping in the womb: cf. *Isaac prayed to the LORD for his wife, because she was barren; and the LORD granted his prayer, and his wife Rebekah conceived. The children struggled together within her; and she said, 'If it is to be this way, why do I live?' So she went to inquire of the LORD. And the LORD said to her, 'Two nations are in your womb, and two peoples born of you shall be divided; the one shall be stronger than the other, the elder shall serve the younger.'* (Genesis 25:21–23)

(V. 42)
A double beatitude, behind which stand the Old Testament references above. This is not a blessing, but a beatitude, just to be clear.

(V. 43)
'My Lord' means that Jesus is already proclaimed Lord. It is by the inspiration of the Holy Spirit that Elizabeth recognises the moment of salvation. The Gospel of Luke will close with other 'visits' of the *risen* Lord.

(V. 44)
The reason for the leaping is given: sheer joy in salvation, a key theme in Luke–Acts.

(V. 45)

The contrast is with Zechariah who did not believe and was struck dumb. Mary did believe and gives her great canticle *before* Zechariah gives his. This is a key verse for the Lucan theology of Mary as model disciple. Cf. Luke 8:19–21; 11:27–28; Acts 1:14. Note that the omission of 'in his own house' in Luke 4:24, in considerable contrast with Mark 6:4, honours this acknowledgement of Jesus 'in his own house'.

Pointers for prayer

a) The greeting of Elizabeth to Mary, 'Blessed are you among women and blessed is the fruit of your womb', is a joyful welcome of the child to come. Bringing new life into the world through pregnancy and birth is one of the most awesome human experiences. How have you experienced this for yourself or in someone close to you?

b) The image of the pregnant Mary going a distance to visit her cousin is a symbol of willingness to look beyond one's own needs to the needs of others. When have you witnessed that kind of generosity in others, or have been able to act in this way yourself?

c) Mary is praised for her faith, because she believed the promise made to her by the Lord would be fulfilled. In what ways have you experienced blessings from your faith and trust in God's promises?

Prayer

Who are we, Lord God, that you should come to us? Yet you have visited your people and redeemed us in your Son.

As we prepare to celebrate his birth, make our hearts leap for joy at the sound of your Word, and move us by your Spirit to bless your wonderful works.

We ask this through him whose day draws near: your Son, Jesus Christ, who lives and reigns with you in the unity of the Holy Spirit, God, for ever and ever. Amen.

🌿 Second reading 🌿

Heb 10:1 *Since the law has only a shadow of the good things to come and not the true form of these realities, it can never, by the same sacrifices that are continually offered year after year, make perfect those who approach.* ² *Otherwise, would they not have ceased being offered, since the worshippers, cleansed once for all, would no longer have any consciousness of sin?* ³ *But in these sacrifices there is a reminder of sin year after year.* ⁴ *For it is impossible for the blood of bulls and goats to take away sins.*

⁵ Consequently, when Christ came into the world, he said, 'Sacrifices and offerings you have not desired, but a body you have prepared for me; ⁶ in burnt offerings and sin offerings you have taken no pleasure. ⁷ Then I said, 'See, God, I have come to do your will, O God (in the scroll of the book it is written of me).'

⁸ When he said above, 'You have neither desired nor taken pleasure in sacrifices and offerings and burnt offerings and sin offerings' (these are offered according to the law), ⁹ then he added, 'See, I have come to do your will.' He abolishes the first in order to establish the second. ¹⁰ And it is by God's will that we have been sanctified through the offering of the body of Jesus Christ once for all.

Initial observations

The reading is probably chosen because of the sense of arrival (*I have come to do your will*), thus making it suitable for the season of Advent. Although it might feel a bit out of season to be talking about the sacrifice of Jesus, in reality Hebrews makes a significant link between the incarnation (the term is not used) and salvation. The opening verses of Hebrews are the second reading for the day Mass of Christmas (see below). The writer depends on this true humanity of Jesus for his teaching on salvation. Jesus can help us because he is like us (see below).

Kind of writing

The Letter to the Hebrews shows the following sequence (according to Albert Vanhoye SJ):

1:1–4	Introduction
1:5–14	Exposition
2:1–4	*Exhortation*
2:5–5:10	Exposition
5:11–6:20	*Exhortation*
7:1–10:18	Exposition
10:19–39	*Exhortation*
11:1–40	Exposition
12:1–13	*Exhortation*
12:14–13:19	*Exhortation*
13:20–25	Conclusion

In an intriguing way, the writer alternates between exposition (straight doctrinal teaching) and exhortation (moral advice). Our reading comes from the key teaching section, 7:1–10:18.

Origin of the reading

The Temple in Jerusalem had been destroyed before this letter was written. Like other Jewish groups, the Christians asked themselves where is the point of access now to the presence of God. Hebrews gives a profound answer, not unlike what you might find in Paul or even in the Gospel of John. A citation from John may serve to illustrate.

Jesus answered them, 'Destroy this Temple, and in three days I will raise it up.' The Jews then said, 'This Temple has been under construction for forty–six years, and will you raise it up in three days?'

But he was speaking of the temple of his body. (John 2:19–21; NB also John 4:21–23)

Related passages

Long ago God spoke to our ancestors in many and various ways by the prophets, but in these last days he has spoken to us by a Son, whom he appointed heir of all things, through whom he also created the worlds. He is the reflection of God's glory and the exact imprint of God's very being, and he sustains all things by his powerful word. When he had made purification for sins, he sat down at the right hand of the Majesty on high, having become as much superior to angels as the name he has inherited is more excellent than theirs. (Hebrews 1:1–4)

Therefore he had to become like his brothers and sisters in every respect, so that he might be a merciful and faithful high priest in the service of God, to make a sacrifice of atonement for the sins of the people. Because he himself was tested by what he suffered, he is able to help those who are being tested. (Hebrews 2:17–18)

Since, then, we have a great high priest who has passed through the heavens, Jesus, the Son of God, let us hold fast to our confession. For we do not have a high priest who is unable to sympathise with our weaknesses, but we have one who in every respect has been tested as we are, yet without sin. Let us therefore approach the throne of grace with boldness, so that we may receive mercy and find grace to help in time of need. (Hebrews 4:14–16)

Brief commentary

(Vv. 5–7)
Psalm 40:6–7 in the Septuagint is significantly different from the Hebrew text. Key manuscripts (e.g. Codex Sinaiticus) read 'a *body* you

have prepared for me' instead of the obscure '*ears* you have prepared for me'. The 'scroll of the book' is shorthand for saying the Scriptures point to Christ.

(V.8)
It is Old Testament teaching that God prefers obedience and observance of the law within the heart (1 Samuel 15:22; Psalm 50:8–10; Isaiah 1:10–13; Jeremiah 7:21–24; Hosea 6:6; Amos 5:21–26) to sacrifice. The inner movement of the heart is more important than the external Temple services.

(V.9)
The contrast is read to mean that the Temple system has been set aside. This is part of a larger argument that the previous system was only a shadow, not the reality. Repetition implies imperfection in contrast with Jesus' offering 'once for all'. The true sacrifice of Jesus is not a blood sacrifice but a movement of the heart, his faithfulness. There is a considerable risk of supersessionism in Hebrews.

(V.10)
This is a very tight summary of the teaching of Hebrews. Contrary to what might seem evident, Jesus' death both abolished and fulfilled Old Testament 'types'. For us, this means salvation and sanctification. Note that 'body' is taken up again (from Psalm 40), but also reminding us of the concrete, costly 'listening' of Jesus in his death on the cross. Listening (*akouō*) and obeying (*hupakouō*) are very similar in Greek.

Pointers for prayer

a) The contrasts may speak to my own experience: outward versus inward worship, temporary versus lasting.

b) Jesus' obedience – that is, deep listening – challenges me to review my own reality as a 'hearer of the word'.

c) 'See, I have come to do your will' could also be a description of the true disciple on the model of Jesus himself.

Prayer

O God, in the faithful obedience of Jesus we see your own faithfulness,
compassion and love. Help us to be faithful to you, to embrace your will for
us and to say with Jesus, 'I have come to do your will.' Through Christ our
Lord. Amen.

🌿 First reading 🌿

Mic 5:2 But you, O Bethlehem of Ephrathah,
who are one of the little clans of Judah,
from you shall come forth for me
one who is to rule in Israel,
whose origin is from of old,
from ancient days.
3   Therefore he shall give them up until the time
when she who is in labour has brought forth;
then the rest of his kindred shall return
to the people of Israel.
4   And he shall stand and feed his flock in the strength of the LORD,
in the majesty of the name of the LORD his God.
And they shall live secure, for now he shall be great
to the ends of the earth;
5   and he shall be the one of peace.

Initial observations

With Christmas just around the corner, it is easy to see why this reading
was chosen. Naturally, even such a reading had a meaning in its historical
context. It is important to establish this before going on to look at the
reception of this oracle in Christian tradition.

Kind of writing

The passage chosen – of obscure origin – speaks, in a highly idealised
fashion, of a future ruler, of the line of David: an oracle.

Origin of the reading

The opening words of the Book of Micah can help us here: *The word of the* LORD *that came to Micah of Moresheth in the days of Kings Jotham, Ahaz, and Hezekiah of Judah, which he saw concerning Samaria and Jerusalem.* (Micah 1:1) Micah was an eighth-century BC prophet from Judah.

The book as a whole has the following structure:

I. Superscription	(1:1)
II. Punishment	(1:2–3:12)
III. Hope	(4:1–5:15 [= in Hebrew 5:14])
IV. Restoration	(6:1–7:20)

Our section comes from section III on hope, dealing with promises to David and his family.

The book as a whole can be quite difficult to read, coming from differing settings and times. It is often thought that our chapter 5, for example, comes from a later period of the late Judahite monarchy, under the inspiration of the Deuteronomistic reforms (see related passages below).

Related passages

> Then all the people who were at the gate, along with the elders, said, 'We are witnesses. May the LORD make the woman who is coming into your house like Rachel and Leah, who together built up the house of Israel. May you produce children in Ephrathah and bestow a name in Bethlehem; and, through the children that the LORD will give you by this young woman, may your house be like the house of Perez, whom Tamar bore to Judah.' (Ruth 4:11–12)

> A shoot shall come out from the stump of Jesse, and a branch shall grow out of his roots. (Isaiah 11:1)

> Now why do you cry aloud? Is there no king in you? Has your counsellor perished, that pangs have seized you like a woman in labour? Writhe and groan, O daughter Zion, like a woman in labour; for now you shall go forth from the city and camp

in the open country; you shall go to Babylon. There you shall be rescued, there the LORD will redeem you from the hands of your enemies. (Micah 4:9–10)

On that day the remnant of Israel and the survivors of the house of Jacob will no more lean on the one who struck them, but will lean on the lord, the Holy One of Israel, in truth. A remnant will return, the remnant of Jacob, to the mighty God. (Isaiah 10:20–21; cf. Isaiah 66:7–8 Ezekiel 34:23–24)

Brief commentary

(V. 2)

Fidelity to David's line is the key here, thus profiling God's faithfulness. 'From of old' suggests that the ancestors were some considerable time ago, so this may be one of the more recent parts of Micah. In Hebrew: *from you for me one will go out to be a ruler over Israel.* Without naming David explicitly, the reading clearly alludes to him. The hope is that another 'David' may usher in a new period of restored national glory.

(V. 3)

This verse seems to reflect on exile, interpreted as punishment and the promise of a return. The language is somewhat apocalyptic on account of the image of labour pains. It is the people, so to speak, who are in labour, not an individual person. Cf. Micah 4:9–10 above. 'The rest of his kindred' are fellow Judahites. Northern tribes are referred to as the 'people of Israel'. In an idealised future, these two should be reunited.

(V. 4)

This promise uses already venerable images of shepherding, an ancient tradition with clear links to the Davidic monarchy. 'He shall be great' is cited in Luke's Gospel: *He will be great, and will be called the Son of the Most High, and the Lord God will give to him the throne of his ancestor David* (Luke 1:32).

(V. 5)

As always, peace has a rich resonance in the Bible: well-being, prosperity, fecundity. There is, perhaps, a late echo of this in Ephesians: *For he is our peace; in his flesh he has made both groups into one and has broken down the dividing wall, that is, the hostility between us* (Ephesians 2:14).

Pointers for prayer

a) Peace – the gift of the Messiah. When have I been at peace myself? Am I a source of peace to others?

b) Flock – Jesus cares for us. Who has cared for me? Who cares for me today? When have I myself known the loving care of God in my life?

c) Time – *For while we were still helpless, at the right time Christ died for the ungodly* (Romans 5:6). Time seems to be a uniquely human experience. Only we notice the passage of time; we realise that the present moment is fleeting; we know there are special moments that remain present to us even after time has marched on.

Prayer

Loving and gracious God, we thank you for the gifts you give us in Jesus your Son: faith, hope and love. Deepen our faith; fulfil our hope; open our hearts. Let this Christmas season be for us once more the right time of his coming, so that Christ may be born in our hearts and brought forth again in our lives. Through Christ our Lord. Amen.

Themes across the readings

The usual clear link between the first and third readings is missing here. Instead, there is a link at the level of the Christian reception of Micah, when the shepherd is seen to be Jesus about to be born and who is 'present' also in the gospel. Psalm 80 (79) explores the image of shepherding, thus responding to the final verses of the reading from Micah. The energy in these readings is varied and very attractive, taking us from birth and joy to a wider longing and hope.

Chapter 5

Christmas Eve: Vigil Mass (ABC)

Thought for the day

Tracing origins has always been of interest. Nowadays it is possible to have a sample of your DNA tested to find out more about your genetic history. It can lead to surprises! Jesus had shadows in his genealogy, as is perfectly normal. There is hope, too, in the ancestors: God can write straight with our crooked lines. The shadows are not simply in our past, they are also in each of us now. The great message of the Gospel is that our past does not always have to stalk us – there is total forgiveness and even amnesia in God: *I, I am the one who blots out your rebellious deeds for my sake; your sins I do not remember* (Isaiah 43:25).

Prayer

Help us to accept from you, God, a new name, a new reality in Christ, that we may know your forgiveness and love and be set free from our past sins and faults. Through Christ our Lord. Amen.

Gospel

Mt 1:1 An account of the genealogy of Jesus the Messiah, the son of David, the son of Abraham.

² Abraham was the father of Isaac, and Isaac the father of Jacob, and Jacob the father of Judah and his brothers, ³ and Judah the father of Perez and Zerah by Tamar, and Perez the father of Hezron, and Hezron the father of Aram, ⁴ and

Aram the father of Aminadab, and Aminadab the father of Nahshon, and Nahshon the father of Salmon, [5] and Salmon the father of Boaz by Rahab, and Boaz the father of Obed by Ruth, and Obed the father of Jesse, [6] and Jesse the father of King David.

And David was the father of Solomon by the wife of Uriah, [7] and Solomon the father of Rehoboam, and Rehoboam the father of Abijah, and Abijah the father of Asaph, [8] and Asaph the father of Jehoshaphat, and Jehoshaphat the father of Joram, and Joram the father of Uzziah, [9] and Uzziah the father of Jotham, and Jotham the father of Ahaz, and Ahaz the father of Hezekiah, [10] and Hezekiah the father of Manasseh, and Manasseh the father of Amos, and Amos the father of Josiah, [11] and Josiah the father of Jechoniah and his brothers, at the time of the deportation to Babylon.

[12] And after the deportation to Babylon: Jechoniah was the father of Salathiel, and Salathiel the father of Zerubbabel, [13] and Zerubbabel the father of Abiud, and Abiud the father of Eliakim, and Eliakim the father of Azor, [14] and Azor the father of Zadok, and Zadok the father of Achim, and Achim the father of Eliud, [15] and Eliud the father of Eleazar, and Eleazar the father of Matthan, and Matthan the father of Jacob, [16] and Jacob the father of Joseph the husband of Mary, of whom Jesus was born, who is called the Messiah.

[17] So all the generations from Abraham to David are fourteen generations; and from David to the deportation to Babylon, fourteen generations; and from the deportation to Babylon to the Messiah, fourteen generations.

[18] Now the birth of Jesus the Messiah took place in this way. When his mother Mary had been engaged to Joseph, but before they lived together, she was found to be with child from the Holy Spirit. [19] Her husband Joseph, being a righteous

man and unwilling to expose her to public disgrace, planned to dismiss her quietly. [20] But just when he had resolved to do this, an angel of the Lord appeared to him in a dream and said, 'Joseph, son of David, do not be afraid to take Mary as your wife, for the child conceived in her is from the Holy Spirit. [21] She will bear a son, and you are to name him Jesus, for he will save his people from their sins.' [22] All this took place to fulfil what had been spoken by the Lord through the prophet:

[23] 'Look, the virgin shall conceive and bear a son, and they shall name him Emmanuel', which means, 'God is with us.'

[24] When Joseph awoke from sleep, he did as the angel of the Lord commanded him; he took her as his wife, [25] but had no marital relations with her until she had borne a son; and he named him Jesus.

Initial observations

There is no doubt that the (optional) genealogy is disconcerting for the modern reader/listener. Nevertheless, it was clearly of immense significance to Matthew. By means of it, the evangelist was able to embed the story of Jesus in the story of God's first chosen people. It is likely that Matthew's community had just broken away from 'the synagogue'. At the same time, this community claimed to be in continuity with God's past disclosure to the Jewish people, now brought to completion in Jesus the Messiah. In particular, the figure of Moses (not mentioned here) dominates Matthew's presentation of Jesus, as a mark of continuity and fulfilment.

Kind of writing

There are two kinds of writing here, genealogy and annunciation. The annunciation-type story shows this pattern:

1. appearance of an angel
2. fear and/or prostration

3. reassurance ('do not fear')
4. message
5. objection
6. a sign is given

The pattern is familiar from the Old Testament (*Ishmael* in Genesis 16:7–12, *Isaac* in Genesis 17:1–21; 18:1–12; *Samson* in Judges 13:3–21) but is only partially present here in Matthew.

Old Testament background

The broad Old Testament story is presented schematically using the device of fourteen generations, taking us from Abraham, through David and the Exile to the time of Jesus. In antiquity, evidently, people were unaware of ovulation. As a result, women were omitted from genealogies, so their inclusion here is especially significant. Each one has a story.

Tamar: Genesis 38
Rahab: Joshua 2–6
Ruth: Ruth 1–4
Wife of Uriah (Bathsheba): 2 Samuel 11–12

All four are in some sense irregular, either sexually and/or as foreigners. They prepare for the great 'irregularity' of the virginal conception and look forward, at the same time, to the inclusion of the Gentiles in the new covenant in Jesus. Sinners likewise have a role in God's plan: three of the women are technically sinners, but so are lots of the men, including David himself and Solomon.

(i) Joseph: the name Joseph reminds the aware Bible reader of another Joseph in the Book of Genesis.

(ii) Divorce was allowed by inference in Deuteronomy 24:4, although no biblical legislation formally permitted it.

(iii) Son of David: the relationship with David immediately calls to mind the guarantee and promise to the house of David made by the prophet Nathan in 2 Samuel 7 and the prayer version of it in Psalm 89.

(iv) Jesus is the Greek for Joshua, the name of Moses' successor, who actually led the people into the promised land. The name comes from Hebrew/Aramaic and means 'YHWH is salvation' or 'YHWH saves/has saved'. As early Christians read the book of Joshua in Greek, they kept hearing the name Jesus/Joshua.

(v) The promise in Isaiah 7:14 is read as a messianic prophecy. In its original context, this text promised a successor to King Ahaz, born in the normal way.

(vi) Communication in a dream: the clear prototypes are Jacob (and his famous ladder) and Joseph (with his coat of many colours).

New Testament foreground

Now the eleven disciples went to Galilee, to the mountain to which Jesus had directed them. When they saw him, they worshipped him; but some doubted. And Jesus came and said to them, 'All authority in heaven and on earth has been given to me. Go therefore and make disciples of all nations, baptising them in the name of the Father and of the Son and of the Holy Spirit, and teaching them to obey everything that I have commanded you. And remember, *I am with you always*, to the end of the age.' (Matthew 28:16–20)

St Paul

For this reason it is by faith so that it may be by grace, with the result that the promise may be certain to all the descendants – not only to those who are under the law, but also to those who have the faith of Abraham, who is the father of us all (as it is written, 'I have made you the father of many nations'). He is our father in the presence of God whom he believed – the God who makes the dead alive and summons the things that do not yet exist as though they already do. Against hope Abraham believed in hope with the result that he became the father of many nations according to the pronouncement, 'so will your descendants be.' Without being weak in faith, he considered his own body as dead (because he was about one hundred years old) and the deadness of Sarah's womb. He did not waver in unbelief about the promise of God but was strengthened in faith, giving glory to God. (Romans 4:16–20)

Brief commentary

Because of the extended Old Testament background, only selected verses will be commented.

(V.1)
The first verse anticipates the threefold pattern, pointing to Jesus.

(V. 6)
People did look back on the time of David as a sort of golden age and many hopes were expressed using Davidic imagery from the Psalms and other early Jewish documents.

(V. 11)
The Babylonian Exile was a watershed in the history and imagination of the Jewish people. It will be referred to again in the slaughter of the innocents in Matthew 2:17–18.

(V. 16)
The pairing of a later Jacob with the later Joseph intentionally echoes the great patriarch, the father of Joseph, one of the twelve sons of Jacob, the progenitors of the twelve tribes of Israel.

(V. 17)
The writer insistently draws our attention to the pattern of fourteen. It may be significant that the consonants of the name David had the numerical value of fourteen in Hebrew.

(V. 18)
Mary was not descended from any of these people, but Joseph, as the legal father of Jesus, was. Betrothal was almost marriage; it was quite in

order, therefore, to speak of divorce. The virginal conception is found also in Luke's account of the conception of Jesus.

(V. 20)
Do not be afraid is a key element in the annunciation-type scene.

(V. 21)
As explained above the name Jesus means YHWH saves. In antiquity, names were regarded as key to the person's identity and mission (cf. '*nomen omen*').

(Vv. 22–23)
Matthew peppers his account with fulfilment citations, of which this is the first. Originally, Isaiah 7:14 (in Hebrew) meant that a wife in the royal family would have a baby in the usual way. Matthew chose the Greek Old Testament (the Septuagint or the LXX), which speaks of a virgin conceiving, but again in the usual way. God-with-us will have a long echo in the gospel.

(Vv. 24–25)
Joseph is always obedient (and silent) in Matthew 1–2. Thus we learn that Jesus is a descendent of David. He will save the people from their sins and will be God-with-us.

Pointers for prayer

a) Every family tree casts shadows, shadows that can overshadow later generations. What have you learned about yourself from your family history?

b) In the narrative, Joseph faces a very challenging situation with a combination of kindness and logic, only to have both set aside by the surprise of God. Have you had that experience too?

c) God-with-us is a powerful expression, inviting me to reflect on my own experience of God with me in my life. Can I name any important moments of God's presence?

d) Every birth is a blessing – even my own! Am I still a blessing to those around me?

Prayer

God of Abraham and Sarah, of David and his descendants, unwearied is your love for us and steadfast is your covenant; wonderful beyond words is your gift of the Saviour, born of the Virgin Mary.

Count us among the people in whom you delight, and by this night's marriage of earth and heaven draw all generations into the embrace of your love.

We ask this through Jesus Christ, your Word made flesh, who lives and reigns with you in the unity of the Holy Spirit, in the splendour of eternal light, God for ever and ever. Amen.

🌿 Second Reading 🌿

Acts 13:16 So Paul stood up, gestured with his hand and said, 'Men of Israel, and you Gentiles who fear God, listen: [17] The God of this people Israel chose our ancestors and made the people great during their stay as foreigners in the country of Egypt, and with uplifted arm he led them out of it. [18] For a period of about forty years he put up with them in the wilderness. [19] After he had destroyed seven nations in the land of Canaan, he gave his people their land as an inheritance. [20] All this took about four hundred fifty years. After this he gave them judges until the time of Samuel the prophet. [21] Then they asked for a king, and God gave them Saul son of Kish, a man from the tribe of Benjamin, who ruled forty years. [22] After removing him, God raised up David their king. He testified about him: 'I have found David the son of Jesse to be a man after my heart, who will accomplish everything I want him to do.' [23] From the descendants of this man God brought to Israel a Saviour, Jesus, just as he promised. [24] Before Jesus arrived, John had proclaimed a baptism for repentance to all the people of Israel. [25] But while John was completing his mission, he said repeatedly, 'What do you think I am? I am not he. But look, one is coming after me. I am not worthy to untie the sandals on his feet!'

Initial observations

This unexpected and yet appropriate reading from the Acts of the Apostles places both John the Baptist and Jesus in the context of Israelite history. The mention of John in the vigil mass of Christmas resumes his role in the time of Advent and, at the same time, makes a bridge between the time of Advent and the present feast of Christmas.

Kind of writing

Fully fifty per cent of the Acts of the Apostles is made up of sermons, discourses and letters. For example, speeches are given by Stephen, Cornelius, James, Gamaliel, Demetrius, Tertullus and Festus. In addition, Peter makes eight speeches, while Paul makes no fewer than nine (Acts 13:16–41; 14:15–17; 17:22–31; 20:18–35; 22:1–21; 24:10–21; 26:2–23, 25–27; 27:21–26; 28:17–20). While the speeches and sermons are adapted to the occasion and characters, we are really hearing Luke's theology of salvation history here. In the history writing of the time, it was up to the author to place appropriate speeches on the lips of the protagonists. As this is the very first of Paul's speeches, the first time we hear his 'voice', it is in some way foundational and so especially important. It would be good to read the whole passage.

Origin of the reading

There are three large issues at stake here.

(i) John the Baptist was a continued source of anxiety even for so late a gospel as Luke's. The evangelist goes to great trouble to 'locate' him in Luke 1–2 and to make sure we see him as the forerunner of Jesus.

(ii) The figure of David – a symbol of God's faithful across time to the people of Israel – was important for early Christianity and, evidently, for Jesus himself. Not only are we supposed to recall 2 Samuel 7, but David was seen as the author of the Psalms. In that capacity, early Christianity saw him as a prophet, foreseeing the time of the Messiah.

(iii) The Gospel of Luke and the Acts may have been written at a time when some Christians were rejecting the Jewish roots of the Christian project. Later in the second century, Marcion (a priest in Rome) challenged the use of Old Testament – he may have been the first but he was certainly not the last! The evangelist is very concerned, in both the gospel and the Acts, to show continuity as a symbol of God's faithfulness through time.

Related pasages

'Brothers, the scripture had to be fulfilled that the Holy Spirit foretold through *David* concerning Judas – who became the guide for those who arrested Jesus – for he was counted as one of us and received a share in this ministry.' (Acts 1:16–17)

But regarding the fact that he has raised Jesus from the dead, never again to be in a state of decay, God has spoken in this way: 'I will give you the holy and trustworthy promises made to *David*.' (Acts 13:34)

For David, after he had served God's purpose in his own generation, died, was buried with his ancestors, and experienced decay, but the one whom God raised up did not experience decay. (Acts 13:36–37)

The Lord declares to you that he himself will build a dynastic house for you. When the time comes for you to die, I will raise up your descendant, one of your own sons, to succeed you, and I will establish his kingdom. (2 Samuel 7:11–12)

Once and for all I have vowed by my own holiness, I will never deceive David. His dynasty will last forever. His throne will endure before me, like the sun, it will remain stable, like the moon, his throne will endure like the skies.' (Psalm 89:35–37)

Brief commentary

(V. 16)
Paul addresses two distinct groups: fellow Jews and 'god-fearers', that is Gentiles attracted to Judaism. The second group is known from literature and from archaeology and may have been drawn to Judaism on account of its pure monotheism, high ethics and noble antiquity.

(V. 17)
Paul cannot tell the story of Jesus without reference to the central story of the Pentateuch, the Exodus. The use of the third person (they) is revealing about the time of writing, already indicating some level of detachment.

(Vv. 18–21)
These verses are omitted for reasons of brevity but are essential for the coherence of the whole story.

(V. 22)
Paul is made to abbreviate the familiar and wonderful story of the search for a successor to Saul. David is praised extravagantly: *a man after my heart, who will carry out all my wishes.*

(V. 23)
The promise takes us back to 2 Samuel 7 and Psalm 89 (see above).

(V. 24)
This is a summary of both Luke 1–2 and Luke 3:1–17.

(V. 25)

This fits with the way Luke has timed the baptism of Jesus in his gospel: Luke 3:19–21. It is made clear for the nth time that John is not the Messiah.

Pointers for prayer

a) Each of us has a story but it is never just our own. On the contrary, we are part of a stream, a continuity. My story, too, is embedded in the generations before me, in the Christian story, and that story is itself embedded in the story of Israel.

b) God wants all of us to be people 'after my heart, who will carry out all my wishes'. What do I do to make my heart transparent to the will of God?

c) The sense of preparation and excitement is tangible as Christmas comes around. What are my hopes this year?

Prayer

May we feel this year, O Lord, the passion and longing of John the Baptist and so prepare ourselves to mark the birth of Jesus, son of David, Son of Man, Son of God, who lives and reigns for ever and ever. Amen.

🌿 First Reading 🌿

Is 62:1 'For the sake of Zion I will not be silent;
for the sake of Jerusalem I will not be quiet,
until her vindication shines brightly
and her deliverance burns like a torch.'
2   Nations will see your vindication,
and all kings your splendour.
You will be called by a new name
that the LORD himself will give you.
3   You will be a majestic crown in the hand of the LORD,
a royal turban in the hand of your God.

⁴ You will no longer be called, 'Abandoned,'
   and your land will no longer be called 'Desolate.'
   Indeed, you will be called 'My Delight is in Her,'
   and your land 'Married.'
   For the LORD will take delight in you,
   and your land will be married to him.
⁵ As a young man marries a young woman,
   so your sons will marry you.
   As a bridegroom rejoices over a bride,
   so your God will rejoice over you.

Initial observations

Our readings open with a passage full of joy and hope, very suitable for the season. It is not quite unfettered happiness but at the same time it is a thrilling passage. The psalm going with the reading joins the uplifting vision of Isaiah with more traditional hopes rooted in God's faithfulness to David and his dynasty. As a result the psalm, rather than the Isaiah reading, sets up the imagery that will be important for both the Acts and for Matthew.

Kind of writing

Isaiah 62 is a prayer for the restoration of Jerusalem, which really runs from Isaiah 61:10 until 62:12. Our excerpt shows clearly the use of 'twin lines' or parallelism, so much part of the energy and power of biblical poetry.

Origin of the reading

Our passage is taken from Third Isaiah and was written most likely in the years after the return from Exile, following the arrival of Cyrus of Persia in 539 BC. Hopes were high after the exiles came back but the reconstruction was frustratingly slow. Accordingly, the prophet gives a great message of hope, to encourage the despondent. Some of the pain is found even in this happy poem: forsaken and desolate. It is evident that much remained to be achieved.

The reading is, nevertheless, very fitting for the vigil Mass of Christmas on account of the tone of expectation combined with sheer joy, spilling over into the exuberant.

Related passages

Indeed, the LORD will call you back like a wife who has been abandoned and suffers from depression, like a young wife when she has been rejected,' says your God. (Isaiah 54:6)

The LORD has proclaimed to the end of the earth: Say to daughter Zion, 'See, your salvation comes; his reward is with him, and his recompense before him.' They shall be called, 'The Holy People, The Redeemed of the LORD'; and you shall be called, 'Sought Out, A City Not Forsaken.' (Isaiah 62:11–12)

Brief commentary

(V. 1a)
The prophet is unable to keep silent. The parallel lines are uneasily synonymous: Zion is part of Jerusalem; 'keep silent' becomes 'rest'.

(V. 1b)
Note how vindication (= God acting justly) and salvation are in parallel. At dawn, the day has broken, but the burning torch suggests it is still night. So, not quite there yet!

(V. 2a)
The parallel lines shift now from vindication to glory, that is, to the public acknowledgement of God's action.

(V. 2b)
In the culture, a change of name is a change of being or relationship ('*nomen omen*'). The parallelism is interrupted to give the origin of the new name: God himself. Cf. *One will say, 'I belong to the LORD,' and another will use the name 'Jacob.' One will write on his hand, 'The LORD's,' and use the name 'Israel'* (Isaiah 44:5).

(V. 3)

Royal symbolism is used, facilitating the change of focus in the psalm to David.

(V. 4a)

The true feelings and experiences of the listeners come to expression. Cf. 'Zion said, 'The Lord has abandoned me, the sovereign master has forgotten me' (Isaiah 49:14).'Indeed, the Lord will call you back like a wife who has been abandoned and suffers from depression, like a young wife when she has been rejected,' says your God (Isaiah 54:6).

(V. 4b–c)

V. 4a is turned around and robustly positive language is used. Cf. *Jerusalem will bring me joy, and my people will bring me happiness. The sound of weeping or cries of sorrow will never be heard in her again* (Isaiah 65:19). V. 4b is 'activated' so to speak in 4c. It is not just a change of name but a change of reality, of being, of heart.

(V. 5a)

The parallelism is evident. Why builder? A more literal translation runs as follows: *As a youth espouses a maiden, Your sons shall espouse you* (Isaiah 62:5, Jewish Publication Society Translation). In Hebrew, the word 'son' is related to the verb 'to build'. Respecting the parallelism, evidently, the New Jerusalem Bible translates thus: *Like a young man marrying a virgin, your rebuilder will wed you, and as the bridegroom rejoices in his bride, so will your God rejoice in you* (Isaiah 62:5, New Jerusalem Bible).

(V. 5b)

This is an uncommon and unexpected metaphor. It reminds one of Psalm 19: *In the sky he has pitched a tent for the sun. Like a bridegroom it emerges from its chamber; like a strong man it enjoys running its course* (Psalm 19:4–5).

Pointers for prayer

a) We do not often think of God as 'rejoicing', much less rejoicing over us or even over me. We touch the heart of the incarnation: 'Thus we are writing these things so that our joy may be complete' (1 John 1:4).

b) Not being able to hold it in was also the experience of Jeremiah (6:11). Do I feel any such 'compulsion' to let others into the secret?

Prayer

God, truly you rejoice in yourself, in your cosmos and even in each one of us. Teach us to live by such conviction that our faith may be truly alive and that others may be drawn to life abundant. Through Christ our Lord. Amen.

Themes across the readings

The figure of David in the psalm, second reading and gospel brings all these readings together. The fidelity of God to the Davidic dynasty symbolises God's faithfulness to us all across time. That faithfulness reaches a new stage in Jesus, a descendant of David. As Christ-believers, we are invited to look back over the major stages and events in our own lives and see how God has always been there for us.

Chapter 6

Christmas Eve: Midnight Mass (ABC)

Thought for the day

The birth of any child is always a source of wonder, when we feel closer to the mystery of life and, in a most natural way, the mystery of God is brought near. In the birth of Jesus, we see our God made visible and so are caught up in love of the God we cannot see. The thrilling reality of the Word made flesh is both gift and call. In the words of the first letter of John, *Beloved, since God loved us so much, we also ought to love one another* (1 John 4:11). We are challenged to love the God we cannot see in the neighbour we can see. There can be no separation of these two realities: to love God is to love your neighbour and to love your neighbour is to love God.

Prayer

Today love itself became flesh like one of us, so that you, O God, might see and love in us what you see and love in him. May we see you and love you in our brothers and sisters. Through Christ our Lord. Amen.

🌿 Gospel 🌿

Lk 2:1 In those days a decree went out from Emperor Augustus that all the world should be registered. [2] This was the first registration and was taken while Quirinius was governor of Syria. [3] All went to their own towns to be registered. [4] Joseph also went from the town of Nazareth in Galilee to Judea, to the city of David called Bethlehem, because he was descended from the house and family of David. [5] He went to be registered with Mary, to whom he was engaged and who was expecting a child. [6] While they were there, the time came for her to deliver her child. [7] And she gave birth to her firstborn son and wrapped him in bands of cloth, and laid him in a manger, because there was no place for them in the inn.

[8] In that region there were shepherds living in the fields, keeping watch over their flock by night. [9] Then an angel of the Lord stood before them, and the glory of the Lord shone around them, and they were terrified. [10] But the angel said to them, 'Do not be afraid; for see – I am bringing you good news of great joy for all the people: [11] to you is born this day in the city of David a Saviour, who is the Messiah, the Lord. [12] This will be a sign for you: you will find a child wrapped in bands of cloth and lying in a manger.' [13] And suddenly there was with the angel a multitude of the heavenly host, praising God and saying, [14] 'Glory to God in the highest heaven, and on earth peace among those whom he favours!'

Initial observations

The birth stories of Jesus are found only in Matthew and Luke, as is well known. Like all gospel stories, they are written retrospectively in the light of the resurrection. Again, just as in the Prologue of John, they serve to provide a Christological key to the identity of Jesus in the rest of the narrative. Finally, again as in the Prologue, they establish a significant level of continuity with the revelation to God's first chosen people.

Both Matthew and Luke write in dialogue with patterns and personalities from the Old Testament and, to a high degree, the writing is determined by those earlier models. While there is indeed a historical core (the Holy Family, Nazareth, Bethlehem, Jerusalem, Herod), nevertheless these accounts are 'parabolic' (even *haggadic*) in nature, rather than straight history as we would understand it today.

Kind of writing

In the context of the culture, this is 'historical' writing, mirroring the conventions and practices of the time. In such cases, the writers use commonplaces to express the significance of the person being written about. The goal is to proclaim the present, living Jesus, not merely to represent the past.

Two backgrounds need to be considered, Jewish and Greco-Roman.

(i) *Midrashic* commentary was a form of filling in the gaps, answering questions that the Scripture itself did not make clear. Accordingly, we might consider certain of the apocryphal writings under the same rubric.

The Greek works of Philo and Josephus (especially in his *Jewish Antiquities*) also expand the biblical text, fill in gaps, allegorise and otherwise interpret the Bible in ways reminiscent of the rabbis. Many of the traditions that these Jews quote in their interpretations of Jewish Scripture find parallels in rabbinic *midrash*.

Neither Matthew 1–2 nor Luke 1–2 is strictly *midrash*, however. *Haggadah* was another kind of devotional writing designed to instruct and uplift. The strong links to biblical models and motifs lend a very strong biblical air to the writing.

(ii) In Greco-Roman culture, the birth of a ruler is sometimes celebrated with a list of his (future) benefits to all humanity. For example, the Priene Calendar Inscription includes some breathtaking affirmations about Augustus, the first emperor:

Since providence, which has divinely disposed our lives, having employed zeal and ardour, has arranged the most perfect culmination for life by producing Augustus, whom for the benefit of mankind she has filled with excellence, as if she had granted him as a saviour for us and our descendants, a saviour who brought war to an end and set all things in peaceful order, and since with his appearance, Caesar exceeded the hopes of all those who had received good news before us, not only surpassing those who had been benefactors before him, but not even leaving any hope of surpassing him for those who are to come in the future, and since the beginning of the good news on his account for the world was the birthday of a god…

Old Testament background

I was nursed with care in swaddling cloths. (Wisdom 7:4)

An ox recognises its owner, a donkey recognises where its owner puts its food; but Israel does not recognise me, my people do not understand. (Isaiah 1:3)

As for you, Bethlehem Ephrathah, seemingly insignificant among the clans of Judah – from you a king will emerge who will rule over Israel on my behalf, one whose origins are in the distant past. (Micah 5:2)

For a child has been born to us, a son has been given to us. He shoulders responsibility and is called: Extraordinary Strategist, Mighty God, Everlasting Father, Prince of Peace. (Isaiah 9:6)

How delightful it is to see approaching over the mountains the feet of a messenger who announces peace, a messenger who brings good news, who announces deliverance, who says to Zion, 'Your God reigns!' (Isaiah 52:7)

New Testament foreground

Men of Israel, listen to these words: Jesus the Nazarene, a man clearly attested to you by God with powerful deeds, wonders, and miraculous signs that God performed among you through him, just as you yourselves know – this man, who was handed over by the predetermined plan and foreknowledge of God, you executed by nailing him to a cross at the hands of Gentiles. But God raised him up, having released him from the pains of death, because it was not possible for him to be held in its power. (Acts 2:22–24)

St Paul

> From Paul, a slave of Christ Jesus, called to be an apostle, set apart for the gospel of God. This gospel he promised beforehand through his prophets in the holy scriptures, concerning his Son who was a descendant of David with reference to the flesh, who was appointed the Son-of-God-in-power according to the Holy Spirit by the resurrection from the dead, Jesus Christ our Lord. Through him we have received grace and our apostleship to bring about the obedience of faith among all the Gentiles on behalf of his name. You also are among them, called to belong to Jesus Christ. To all those loved by God in Rome, called to be saints: Grace and peace to you from God our Father and the Lord Jesus Christ! (Romans 1:1–7)

Brief commentary

(V.1)

Augustus was the grand-nephew and adopted son of the deified Julius Caesar, and therefore could claim to be a 'son of God', a *dei filius*. On his death in AD 14, Tiberius became emperor. There was no *worldwide* census in the time of Augustus. Luke is mixing it up with a census of Syria, which took place before the death of Archaelaus in AD 6, under the governorship of Quirinius. The solemn beginning resembles Luke 3:1. Augustus was regarded as the saviour of the world and the bringer of the Pax Romana. Luke challenges that, especially in 2:14.

(V. 2)

Publius Sulpicius Quirinius was a real historical figure, from Lanuvio (Lanuvium) not far from Castelgandolfo, who was made legate of Syria in AD 6 with the special task of restructuring Judea as a Roman province.

(V. 3)

There is no evidence for such a disruptive practice. It does, however, echo the instructions for the Jubilee Year, a theme in Luke 4:16–30.

(V. 4)

City of David would normally be taken to be Jerusalem; here, of course, it refers to Bethlehem.

(V. 5)

This is a quick summary of Luke 1:26–38.

(V. 6)

Compare Genesis 25:24 and Luke 1:57.

(V. 7)

Firstborn meant a particular status in the Jewish Law, without prejudice to other children being born. The old word 'swaddle' is a direct echo of Wisdom 7:4, where the whole context is interesting. Solomon, *son of David*, was also wrapped in swaddling clothes. The reference to the manger was filled out in the iconographic tradition to cause an unkind echo of Isaiah 1:3. It can mean a variety of things: a private home, a room, an inn, a space in a stable.

(V. 8)

The shepherd echoes the David tradition. This has also been used to date the actual birth of Jesus to between March and November, when shepherds would be out in the fields. Shepherds were sometimes considered outcasts. Bethlehem: cf. Micah 4–5, especially 5:2 (above).

(V. 9)

Glory: cf. Luke 2:9, 14, 32; 4:6; 9:26, 31–32; 12:27; 14:10; 17:18; 19:38; 21:27; 24:26. Shone: cf. the conversion of St Paul in Acts 26:13, by the same writer.

(V. 10)

'Do not be afraid' is a commonplace of angelic appearances and theophanies. The long English expression 'bring good news' is a single verb in Greek, 'I gospel you', so to speak.

(V. 11)

Today is a favourite expression of Luke. Cf. Luke 2:11; 4:21; 5:26; 12:28; 13:32–33; 19:5, 9; 22:34, 61; 23:43. Saviour is unexpectedly rare in the gospels and Acts: Matthew (x0), Mark (x0), Luke (x2), John (x1), Acts (x2). (Cf. Luke 1:47; 2:11; John 4:42; Acts 5:31; 13:23). Christ the Lord (common in Paul) is rare in the gospels and Acts: Matthew (x0), Mark (x0), Luke (x2), John (x0), Acts (x1).

(V. 12)
Jesus, not Augustus, is the saviour. Cf. Isaiah 9:6 and 52:7.

(V. 13)
Luke regularly underlines the praise of God: Matthew (x0), Mark (x0), Luke (x6), John (x0).

(V. 14)
Glory is the visible manifestation of divine majesty and a strong contrast with the fragility of a newborn baby. Highest heavens, i.e. into the further reaches of heaven, so to speak.

Pointers for prayer

a) Bring to mind a time when the birth of a child made a huge impact on you. Use the experience to meditate upon the birth of Jesus, the incarnation.

b) There is great joy in the gospel tonight. Have you ever felt such spontaneous, exultant happiness? A prayer of praise and thanksgiving.

Prayer

Good and gracious God, on this holy night you gave us your Son, the Lord of the universe, wrapped in swaddling clothes, the Saviour of all, lying in a manger. On this holy night draw us into the mystery of your love. Join our voices with the heavenly host, that we may sing your glory on high.

Give us a place among the shepherds, that we may find the one for whom we have waited, Jesus Christ, your Word made flesh, who lives and reigns with you in the unity of the Holy Spirit, in the splendour of eternal light, God for ever and ever. Amen.

🌿 Second Reading 🌿

Tit 2:11 For the grace of God has appeared, bringing salvation to all people. [12] It trains us to reject godless ways and worldly desires and to live self-controlled, upright, and godly lives in the present age, [13] as we wait for the happy fulfilment of our hope in the glorious appearing of our great God and Saviour, Jesus Christ. [14] He gave himself for us to set us free from every kind of lawlessness and to purify for himself a people who are truly his, who are eager to do good. [15] *So communicate these things with the sort of exhortation or rebuke that carries full authority. Don't let anyone look down on you.*

Initial observations

Our reading is beautifully laid out and teaches us that, as Christians, we live in the in-between time, our lives marked by both memory and hope. It is chosen today because it underlines that salvation is for all, without distinction. The claims about Jesus put the writer on a collision course with the empire (see below).

Many scholars think this letter does not come from the hand of the apostle himself. Titus is a document of the second or even third generation of the Pauline churches.

Kind of writing

The Pastorals present themselves as personal letters from Paul to significant companions. In reality, they are written to communities (in Asia Minor) to bring Pauline doctrine into a new context. They preserve, however, the letter structure from Paul, as in the case of Titus:

1:1–4	Salutation
1:5–3:11	Body of the letter
3:12–15	Travels, greetings, blessing

The body of the letter:

1:5–9	Elders
1:10–16	Warnings
2:1–10	The Christian household
2:11–15	*Appearance of Christ*
3:1–11	To the whole church

For completeness' sake, v. 15 is added (it does capture the different tone of these documents). Some of the resounding vocabulary used here marks the text as *not* from Paul: to appear; saving (= salvation as an adjective); to renounce; worldly; self-controlled (= literally wisely); godly; manifestation; great; to redeem; of his own; to look down on (none of these expressions is ever found in the undisputed letters of Paul).

Origin of the reading

The writer(s) of the Pastorals were facing a variety of threats at the start of the second century. In response, it is true that there is some domestication of the radical Paul, but there is more to it than that.

The letters also represent a development of Pauline doctrine in several directions: (i) spirits, angels and the Holy Spirit; (ii) the Church as the household of God, with great regard for the inspired Jewish Scriptures. The tension towards the end of time found in Paul is abandoned – there will still be a second coming, but it is in the very indefinite future. As for date and place, mostly likely it comes from Asia Minor/Western Turkey, around the year AD 100.

Related passages

> But as for you, continue in what you have learned and firmly believed, knowing from whom you learned it, and how from childhood you have known the sacred writings that are able to instruct you for salvation through faith in Christ Jesus. (2 Timothy 3:14–15)

Paul, a servant of God and an apostle of Jesus Christ, for the sake of the faith of God's elect and the knowledge of the truth that is in accordance with godliness, in the hope of eternal life that God, who never lies, promised before the ages began – in due time he revealed his word through the proclamation with which I have been entrusted by the command of God our Saviour, to Titus, my loyal child in the faith we share: Grace and peace from God the Father and Christ Jesus our Saviour. (Titus 1:1–4)

But when the goodness and loving kindness of God our Saviour appeared, he saved us, not because of any works of righteousness that we had done, but according to his mercy, through the water of rebirth and renewal by the Holy Spirit. This Spirit he poured out on us richly through Jesus Christ our Saviour, so that, having been justified by his grace, we might become heirs according to the hope of eternal life. (Titus 3:4–7)

Brief commentary

(V. 11)
The grace of God is evidently bringing salvation to all; it is not limited to one people (for example, the Jews) or to an elite (for example the Gnostics). At the heart of this first appearance stands the cross and resurrection.

(V. 12)
This pile-up of attitudes teaches us that we are to live truly transformed lives in response to this great grace. The Christmas feast can be cosy and 'harmless'. Taking it earnestly means embarking on a journey of deep change. The Gospel is an all-or-nothing offer of life transformed.

(V. 13)
There will be a second appearance or coming. The Gospel is lived in hope between these events. 'Great God and Saviour' was found in Ephesus in an inscription dedicated to Caesar. For the author of Titus, the Gospel proclaims another great God and Saviour, Jesus Christ.

(V. 14)

There are allusions here to the authentic Paul in Galatians 2:15–21. The 'for us' indicates that not everyone has responded; it is also an echo of the Suffering Servant theme. The biblical language of chosen people etc. is applied here to the Christian community. Again, a transformed life is indicated.

Pointers for prayer

a) At Christmas, once we get beyond the tinsel, we encounter 'the scandalous particularity of the incarnation' at the heart of Christian faith. Who is Jesus in my life? How do I experience his salvation?

b) As we get older, we gradually get used to living in between birth and death; there is for us another in-between: the fact of Christ and the hope we have in him. This is the basis for our transformed living in the present moment.

Prayer

Saving, healing God, you reach out to us in Jesus, bringing light into the darkness of human life. Help us put our hands into his hands, that he may bring us to you.

Grant this through him, whose light has shone, your Son, our Lord Jesus Christ, who lives and reigns with you in the unity of the Holy Spirit, God, for ever and ever. Amen.

First Reading

Is 9:1 *But there will be no gloom for those who were in anguish. In the former time he brought into contempt the land of Zebulun and the land of Naphtali, but in the latter time he will make glorious the way of the sea, the land beyond the Jordan, Galilee of the nations.*

2   The people who walked in darkness
      have seen a great light;
   those who lived in a land of deep darkness –
      on them light has shined.
3   You have multiplied the nation,
      you have increased its joy;
   they rejoice before you
      as with joy at the harvest,
      as people exult when dividing plunder.
4   For the yoke of their burden,
      and the bar across their shoulders,
      the rod of their oppressor,
      you have broken as on the day of Midian.
5   For all the boots of the tramping warriors
      and all the garments rolled in blood
      shall be burned as fuel for the fire.
6   For a child has been born for us,
      a son given to us;
   authority rests upon his shoulders;
      and he is named
Wonderful Counsellor, Mighty God,
      Everlasting Father, Prince of Peace.
7   His authority shall grow continually,
      and there shall be endless peace
for the throne of David and his kingdom.
      He will establish and uphold it
with justice and with righteousness
      from this time onward and forevermore.
The zeal of the LORD of hosts will do this.

Initial observations

This is an especially appropriate and loved reading for Christmas
Midnight Mass and the setting of parts of this text in Handel's *Messiah*
have made it even more familiar and appreciated. The themes of

darkness/light, child and the throne of David fit the feast. Nevertheless, it does come from a particular moment in history and has to be read first of all in its religious and political setting.

Kind of writing

Isaiah 9:2–7 is a prophetic oracle in the form of poetry, reflecting the conventions and techniques of biblical poetry generally. The parallelism is evident, for instance, in vv. 2ab and 2cd. As the verses proceed, there is insistence by sheer force of repetition. Thus, in v. 3, we have joy, rejoice, exult. The suggestion of dividing plunder (after an implied victory) at the end of v. 3 is continued in the military metaphors of vv. 4 and 5. Thus a reversal of a national calamity is envisaged. What has brought this about? The birth of an heir to the family of David. Tremendous hopes are placed on the shoulders of this child. Of course, there is no way of knowing that a child would have been able to achieve all this. Instead, the birth is taken to be a mark of God's continued fidelity to the house of David, and the salvation of God will be the work of God himself. In all the colourful imagery in vv.6–7, important words are profiled: peace, justice, righteousness.

Origin of the reading

As noted elsewhere, the present Book of Isaiah reflects three distinct periods. The original Isaiah of Jerusalem was active from about 738 BC (Isaiah 6:1) until 701 BC, perhaps until 687/6 BC, so it was a considerable ministry of some forty or fifty years. His preaching is preserved in Isaiah 1–39. The period was a time of transition from prosperity and security to insecurity and threat as the Assyrian empire flexed its muscles. In the time of Isaiah, there were several conflicts with Assyria: 743–738, 735–732 (the Syro-Ephraimite war), 714–705 and, finally, 703–701.

Our excerpt comes from the period of the Syro-Ephraimite war. During this time, Isaiah preached the uncomfortable view that the Assyrians, under the marvellously named Tiglath-Pileser III, were an instrument of God, sent to punish and to bring Israel back to true faith in YHWH. Isaiah 1–12 deals with the condemnation of Judah (through Assyria) and

God's offer of salvation through renewed fidelity. The cycles of promise (2–4) and threat (5–11) are interrupted by Isaiah 6:1–9:7, made up of oracles dealing with the Syro-Ephraimite war. This block forms the core of Isaiah 2–12 and provides the theological heart of the chapters. The traditions about Zion and the Davidic monarchy are expounded and explored. The typical pattern is threat, punishment, salvation.

Related passages

Several passages, too long to cite, come to mind: 2 Samuel 7; Isaiah 2:4, 7:14; 11:1–2, 8–9.

> He shall judge between the nations, and shall arbitrate for many peoples; they shall beat their swords into ploughshares, and their spears into pruning hooks; nation shall not lift up sword against nation, neither shall they learn war any more. (Isaiah 2:4)

> Therefore the LORD himself will give you a sign. Look, the young woman is with child and shall bear a son, and shall name him Immanuel (Isaiah 7:14)

> A shoot shall come out from the stump of Jesse, and a branch shall grow out of his roots. The spirit of the LORD shall rest on him, the spirit of wisdom and understanding, the spirit of counsel and might, the spirit of knowledge and the fear of the LORD. The nursing child shall play over the hole of the asp, and the weaned child shall put its hand on the adder's den. They will not hurt or destroy on all my holy mountain; for the earth will be full of the knowledge of the LORD as the waters cover the sea. (Isaiah 11:1–2, 8–9)

Brief commentary

(V.2)
Darkness represents the calamity that has befallen the kingdom of Judah; light is used for deliverance through a new king 'of David's line'.

(V. 3)

God is addressed ('you') and given the credit for the restored community, leading to great rejoicing. A contrast is drawn in which harvest points to the fruits of labour while plunder points to the fruits of conflict already over.

(V. 4)

Note the emphasis: yoke, bar, rod. In Judges 7–8, Gideon's victory over Midian delivered the people from foreign oppression.

(V. 5)

An end to war is pictured here. Cf. *He shall judge between the nations, and shall arbitrate for many peoples; they shall beat their swords into ploughshares, and their spears into pruning hooks; nation shall not lift up sword against nation, neither shall they learn war any more.* (Isaiah 2:4)

(V. 6)

The historical referent is a child born of Davidic ancestry. 'Mighty God' might seem too much for a human being, but the New American Bible translated 'God-hero'. In any case: wisdom, heroism, fatherhood, peace. Prince of peace because the king establishes a safe socio-economic environment for his people.

(V. 7)

Peace is emphasised again. The import of the very last line has been well captured in the New English Translation: *The LORD's intense devotion to his people will accomplish this.* This 'zeal' is a covenant quality of God in relation to Israel.

Pointers for prayer

a) Recall times when you have 'walked in darkness'. What was it like? What helped you to keep going? Was there a turning point, when darkness turned to light?

b) A birth is always a joy! Think back to the joy of your own parents when you yourself arrived in the world. Use this very natural human happiness to come close to the happiness of today's feast.

c) Endless peace sounds great, but, as we know, peace is always 'under construction', always fragile, always in need of support. Where have you experienced peace? What about your own commitment to be a peacemaker, a bearer of peace to others?

Prayer

Loving God, our light and our hope, show yourself once more as our true guide. Teach us to recognise in your Son Jesus love which you alone give, the peace the world cannot give. Through Christ our Lord. Amen.

Themes across the readings

By means of the response, the first reading is read in the light of Jesus' birth and appearing, themes taken up in the second reading and the gospel. There is an air of excitement and joy, of hope finally fulfilled. The thrill of every human birth should help us celebrate the birth of our saviour and the rebirth of us all.

Chapter 7

Christmas Day: Dawn Mass (ABC)

Thought for the day

Sharing the excitement is a very human response. We have all done it at some stage: some great news in the family, perhaps a promotion, or the discovery of a place of spectacular beauty, or some situation that has turned around. The desire to let others know tells us that sharing such experiences is itself part of the original delight. Something similar may be said of the sense of discovery and delight we find in the Good News of Jesus. Like, the prophets of old (Jeremiah 6:19) or like St Paul (1 Corinthians 9:16), we just can't keep it in! We want, we *need* to let others know in order to complete our delight and our sense of discovery.

Prayer

In these days, loving God, give us not only courageous joy but joyful courage to proclaim to others our own delight at the discovery of Good News. May we be bearers of your Word of life to all. Through the same Christ our Lord. Amen.

Gospel

Lk 2:15 When the angels had left them and gone into heaven, the shepherds said to one another, 'Let us go now to Bethlehem and see this thing that has taken place, which the Lord has made known to us.' [16] So they went with haste and found Mary and Joseph, and the child lying in the manger. [17] When they saw this, they made known what had been told them about this child; [18] and all who heard it were amazed at what the shepherds told them. [19] But Mary treasured all these words and pondered them in her heart. [20] The shepherds returned, glorifying and praising God for all they had heard and seen, as it had been told them.

Initial observations

This reading is simply the continuation of the reading for Midnight Mass. Some of the information given there applies here too, of course. It illustrates a response to the events of salvation and already some are worshipping the baby.

Kind of writing

(i) History: In the context of the culture, this is 'historical' writing, mirroring the conventions and practices of the time. In such cases, the writers use standard commonplaces or *topoi* to express the significance of the person being written about. As can be seen in the notes, the history is a bit dodgy and the place given to the miraculous would not count as history today.

(ii) *Midrash*: Neither Matthew 1–2 nor Luke 1–2 is strictly *midrash*, a type of rewriting and filling out of biblical narratives found at the time. However, the strong links to biblical models and motifs lend a kind of midrashic air to the writing.

Old Testament background

(i) *David as shepherd*: When they came, he looked on Eliab and thought, 'Surely the LORD's anointed is now before the LORD.' But the LORD said to Samuel, 'Do not look on his appearance or on the height of his stature, because I have rejected him; for the LORD does not see as mortals see; they look on the outward appearance, but the LORD looks on the heart.' Then Jesse called Abinadab, and made him pass before Samuel. He said, 'Neither has the LORD chosen this one.' Then Jesse made Shammah pass by. And he said, 'Neither has the LORD chosen this one.' Jesse made seven of his sons pass before Samuel, and Samuel said to Jesse, 'The LORD has not chosen any of these.' Samuel said to Jesse, 'Are all your sons here?' And he said, 'There remains yet the youngest, but he is keeping the sheep.' And Samuel said to Jesse, 'Send and bring him; for we will not sit down until he comes here.' He sent and brought him in. Now he was ruddy, and had beautiful eyes, and was handsome. The LORD said, 'Rise and anoint him; for this is the one.' Then Samuel took the horn of oil, and anointed him in the presence of his brothers; and the spirit of the LORD came mightily upon David from that day forward. Samuel then set out and went to Ramah.(1 Samuel 16:6–13)

(ii) *Davidic shepherd to come*: I will set up over them one shepherd, my servant David, and he shall feed them: he shall feed them and be their shepherd.(Ezekiel 34:23)

My servant David shall be king over them; and they shall all have one shepherd. They shall follow my ordinances and be careful to observe my statutes. (Ezekiel 37:24)

(iii) *Bethlehem*: Often mentioned in connection with David (1 Samuel 17:12, 15; 20:6, 28; 2 Samuel 23:14–16; 1 Chronicles 11:16–18; Luke 2:4; John 7:42). A significant echo can also be found in the book of Ruth (Ruth 1:1–2, 19, 22; 2:4; 4:11). The key text, however, is the one cited by Luke:

But you, O Bethlehem of Ephrathah, who are one of the little clans of Judah, from you shall come forth for me one who is to rule in Israel, whose origin is from of old, from ancient days. (Micah 5:2)

New Testament foreground

The Davidic origin of Jesus is important in the New Testament and present in the earliest texts, such as Romans 1:1–7. In the gospels, it is important and present even in John's Gospel. David is also a consistent subject of reflection in Luke's second volume. For example:

> The whole assembly kept silence, and listened to Barnabas and Paul as they told of all the signs and wonders that God had done through them among the Gentiles. After they finished speaking, James replied, 'My brothers, listen to me. Simeon has related how God first looked favourably on the Gentiles, to take from among them a people for his name. This agrees with the words of the prophets, as it is written, 'After this I will return, and I will rebuild the dwelling of David, which has fallen; from its ruins I will rebuild it, and I will set it up, so that all other peoples may seek the Lord – even all the Gentiles over whom my name has been called. Thus says the Lord, who has been making these things known from long ago. (Acts 15:12–19)

> 'And now, friends, I know that you acted in ignorance, as did also your rulers. In this way God fulfilled what he had foretold through all the prophets, that his Messiah would suffer. Repent therefore, and turn to God so that your sins may be wiped out, so that times of refreshing may come from the presence of the Lord, and that he may send the Messiah appointed for you, that is, Jesus, who must remain in heaven until the time of universal restoration that God announced long ago through his holy prophets.' (Acts 3:17–21).

St Paul

Apart from Romans 1:1–7, Paul refers to David as the author of the Psalms.

> So even David himself speaks regarding the blessedness of the man to whom God credits righteousness apart from

works: 'Blessed are those whose lawless deeds are forgiven, and whose sins are covered; blessed is the one against whom the Lord will never count sin.' (Romans 4:6–8)

Brief commentary

(V. 15)
Shepherds as such don't really recur in the gospel. But there is, of course, the parable of the lost sheep in Luke 15:3–7.

(V.16)
Mary and Joseph were previously mentioned in Luke 1:27.

(V. 17)
The word for what had been told them (*rhēma*) is a feature of Luke–Acts: Matthew (x5); Mark (x2); Luke (x9); John (x12); Acts (x14). The range is from 'what was said' to 'an event that can be spoken about'. That is, they bear witness, confirming their experience. Cf. Luke 24:35.

(V. 18)
The 'all' is very important for Matthew and for Luke and on this day means that salvation is offered to all without discrimination or distinction. Here are the occurrences: Matthew (x129); Mark (x69); Luke (x158); John (x65); Acts (x171). Cf. 'In the last days it will be, God declares, that I will pour out my Spirit upon all flesh, and your sons and your daughters shall prophesy, and your young men shall see visions, and your old men shall dream dreams (Acts 2:17).Then Peter began to speak to them: 'I truly understand that God shows no partiality, but in every nation anyone who fears him and does what is right is acceptable to him. You know the message he sent to the people of Israel, preaching peace by Jesus Christ – he is Lord of all (Acts 10:34–37). Amazement as a reaction is also a feature of Luke–Acts: Matthew (x7); Mark (x4); Luke (x13); John (x6); Acts (x5).

(V. 19)
The only two other occurrences of the word 'treasured' illustrate the range of meaning rather well: (i) Neither is new wine put into old wineskins;

otherwise, the skins burst, and the wine is spilled, and the skins are destroyed; but new wine is put into fresh wineskins, and so both are *preserved* (Matthew 9:17). (ii) for Herod feared John, knowing that he was a righteous and holy man, and he *protected* him. When he heard him, he was greatly perplexed; and yet he liked to listen to him (Mark 6:20).

In the New Testament, the other word 'pondered' is limited to Luke–Acts (Luke 2:19; 14:31; Acts 4:15; 17:18; 18:27; 20:14). The meaning ranges from the literal (to take with) to the metaphorical (to consider, to discuss). Heart also has a certain prominence in Luke–Acts: Matthew (x16); Mark (x11); Luke (x22); John (x7); Acts (x20).

(V. 20)

To glorify has a limited frequency in Luke–Acts, but of course it is extensively used in John's Gospel: Matthew (x4); Mark (x1); Luke (x9); John (x23); Acts (x5). The gospel ends with something very like this: and they were continually in the Temple blessing God (Luke 24:53). Praising, even if not that common, is special to Luke–Acts: Matthew (x0); Mark (x0); Luke (x3); John (x0); Acts (x3). 'Seen and heard' is an interesting combination. Cf. And he answered them, 'Go and tell John what you have seen and heard: the blind receive their sight, the lame walk, the lepers are cleansed, the deaf hear, the dead are raised, the poor have good news brought to them (Luke 7:22). Then he said, 'The God of our ancestors has chosen you to know his will, to see the Righteous One and to hear his own voice; for you will be his witness to all the world of what you have seen and heard. And now why do you delay? Get up, be baptised, and have your sins washed away, calling on his name' (Acts 22:14–16).

Pointers for prayer

a) This was no ordinary child. It is the birth of the Son of God. In order to take in the implications of that we can do well to recall Meister Eckhart's reflection and ask ourselves how the birth of Jesus takes place in us: *What good is it to me if the eternal birth of the divine Son takes place unceasingly but does not take place within myself? And what good is it to me if Mary is full of grace and if I am not also full of grace?*

b) The shepherds were both frightened and thrilled. Good news can sometimes be terrifying. Pregnancy and the birth of a child can give rise to both feelings. It is to be hoped that the joy and wonder at new life outweigh the fear and apprehension. What has been your experience?

Prayer

Today, O God of light, your loving kindness dawns, your tender compassion breaks upon us, for in our Saviour, born of human flesh, you reveal your gracious gift of our birth to life eternal.

Fill us with the wonder of this holy day: let us treasure in our hearts what we have been told, that our lives may proclaim your great and gentle mercy.

We make our prayer through Jesus Christ, your Word made flesh, who lives and reigns with you in the unity of the Holy Spirit, in the splendour of eternal light, for ever and ever. Amen.

🌿 Second Reading 🌿

Tit 3:3 *For we ourselves were once foolish, disobedient, led astray, slaves to various passions and pleasures, passing our days in malice and envy, despicable, hating one another.* [4] But when the goodness and loving kindness (*philanthrōpia*) of God our Saviour appeared, [5] he saved us, not because of any works of righteousness that we had done, but according to his mercy, through the water of rebirth and renewal by the Holy Spirit. [6] This Spirit he poured out on us richly through Jesus Christ our Saviour, [7] so that, having been justified by his grace, we might become heirs according to the hope of eternal life. [8] *The saying is sure.*

Initial observations

There are three emphases that make this an attractive reading for Christmas: (i) the loving kindness of God (lit. God's *philanthropy*); (ii) all is gift and grace; (iii) through the Holy Spirit, we too become the sons and daughters of God, coheirs with Christ.

Kind of writing

For the letter layout of Titus, the reader is invited to go back to chapter 6, under the second reading.

The layout of the final chapter is clear:

1–2:	Practical instruction
3–8a:	Theological support
8b–11:	Direct encouragement

The appointed reading is Titus 3:4–7. The omitted vv. 3 and 8 of the central section are included here for completeness and coherence. V. 8a is one of the 'faithful' sayings found in the Pastorals: 1 Timothy 1:15; 3:1; 4:9; 2 Timothy 2:11; and here in Titus 3:8. Here they are in the New English Translation:

> This saying is trustworthy (*pistos*) and deserves full acceptance: Christ Jesus came into the world to save sinners – and I am the worst of them! (1 Timothy 1:15)

> This saying is trustworthy (*pistos*):If someone aspires to the office of overseer, he desires a good work. (1 Timothy 3:1)

> This saying is trustworthy (*pistos*) and deserves full acceptance. (1 Timothy 4:9)

> This saying is trustworthy (*pistos*): If we died with him, we will also live with him. (2 Timothy 2:11)

Origin of the reading

At this point in the letter, the writer is contrasting their past manner of living with their current lives as Christ-believers. V. 3 is rather pungent but vv. 4–7 more than make up for it. In the culture of the day, *philanthrōpia* had a very high value. Our writer uses it not to talk about the kindness of fellow humans – the usual use and always limited – but to talk of God's astonishing kindness us all, which knows no limits.

Related passages

For the *grace* of *God* has *appeared*, bringing *salvation* to all *people* (Titus 2:11).

This passage from Ephesians is remarkably similar to our reading.

> All of us once lived among them in the passions of our flesh, following the desires of flesh and senses, and we were by nature children of wrath, like everyone else. But God, who is rich in mercy, out of the great love with which he loved us even when we were dead through our trespasses, made us alive together with Christ – by grace you have been saved – and raised us up with him and seated us with him in the heavenly places in Christ Jesus, so that in the ages to come he might show the immeasurable riches of his grace in kindness toward us in Christ Jesus. (Ephesians 2:3–7)

> It is not because of your righteousness or the uprightness of your heart that you are going in to occupy their land; but because of the wickedness of these nations the LORD your God is dispossessing them before you, in order to fulfil the promise that the LORD made on oath to your ancestors, to Abraham, to Isaac, and to Jacob. (Deuteronomy 9:5)

Brief commentary

(V. 4)
The goodness of God is a genuinely Pauline expression (e.g. Romans 2:4; 3:12; 11:22). God's 'philanthropy' is rarer, being found only in Acts 28:2. The New Jerusalem Bible gets it right: the kindness and *love* of God our Saviour for *humanity*. To appear and appearance are typical of the vocabulary of later generations. Saviour – oddly rare in the gospels and in Paul – is also an expression of evolving Christianity.

(V. 5a)

This verse is perhaps the clearest statement in all the Bible that salvation is wholly the initiative of God. The sentiment is not anti-Jewish because ancient Israelites/Jews were well aware of their status as the *elect* (see Deuteronomy 9:5 above). It looks like a restatement of Pauline teaching, as long as we remember that the apostle contrasts grace *not with works of righteousness* (good deeds of any kind), but with the *ritual law* (meaning the dietary laws, sabbath observance and circumcision). The writer is also not saying that works don't matter: it is simply affirming that our relationship with God is initiated and sustained by God's grace alone.

(V. 5b–6)

Christians enter this grace through (i) baptism and the gift of the Spirit, (ii) renewal (a word confined to Christian usage) and (iii) Jesus Christ our Saviour. For this writer, Saviour refers first to God the Father as giver and then to Jesus as mediator. The Spirit receives less emphasis in the Pastorals, perhaps reflecting the settling down (institutionalisation) of The Way.

(V. 7)

As the final verse in the lectionary excerpt, these words bring out the goal of the coming of Christ: that we might be heirs with him. Two Pauline themes are reflected here: justification by grace and becoming sons and daughters of God.

Pointers for prayer

a) In the secular celebration of Christmas, the giving of gifts is the defining action. Relationship and love, wonder and gratitude all come into play – and not only in our human interconnectedness but also in God's love affair with humanity.

b) Christmas is a time of rest and refreshment. This is good – yet it would be a pity not to rest in God too and experience refreshment in the faith. What shall *I* do to bring that about?

Prayer

Abba, father and creator, we stand before you, in awe and thankfulness.

As we experience your gracious 'philanthropy', help us to become more and more like you, loving as we have been loved. Thus, may we become ever more truly your sons and daughters. Through Christ our Lord. Amen.

🌿 First Reading 🌿

Is 62:11 Look, the LORD announces to the entire earth:

'Say to Daughter Zion,
'Look, your deliverer comes!
Look, his reward is with him
and his reward goes before him!"

¹² They will be called, 'The Holy People,
the Ones Protected by the LORD.'
You will be called, 'Sought After,
City Not Abandoned.'

Initial observations

The questions being addressed by Third Isaiah have a contemporary ring to them: Could they really believe God had forgiven them? In the light of recent experience, could they count on God's continued protection? Who could possibly be the leader of the community? Even more importantly, how could they so live that they might avoid repeating the sins and errors that brought on them the calamity of the exile in Babylon? All this is not so obvious in the short excerpt chosen for the dawn Mass of Christmas day. Nevertheless, v.11 reflects the idea the salvation is *not yet* a present reality, while v. 12 expresses the feelings still remembered from the Exile – a city *forsaken*.

None of this should take away from the real joy of the reading; but just as there is no cheap grace, there is likewise no cheap joy.

Kind of writing

All of Isaiah 61 is poetry, of course, and these few verses derive their power from the poetry. The typical parallelism is not exact, but the 'uneasy synonymity' (R. Alter) has undoubted energy.

Origin of the reading

As just noted, this reading comes from Third Isaiah, that is, from the final chapters, 56–66. The exiles have returned after the fall of Babylon in 539 and the victory of Cyrus. However, not all have returned, reconstruction is difficult and there is conflict between two groups in the community. The centrepiece of the writing is chapters 60–62, with five units before (Isaiah 56:1–8; 56:9–57:13; 57:14–21; 58; 59) and five units after (Isaiah 63:1–6; 63:7–64:2; 65; 66:1–16; 66:17–24).

Related Passages

(i) Daughter Zion: this term appears twenty-six times in the Old Testament, sometimes in parallel with 'daughter Jerusalem'. It appears in two contexts: disaster and redemption. As an example, reference may be made to the Book of Lamentations (1:6; 2:1, 4, 8, 10, 13, 18; 4:22), and there is a striking example in Jeremiah: *For I heard a cry as of a woman in labour, anguish as of one bringing forth her first child, the cry of daughter Zion gasping for breath, stretching out her hands, 'Woe is me! I am fainting before killers!'* (Jeremiah 4:31).

In these contexts, the language conveys both vulnerability and defilement. In the more positive settings, the language can be quite upbeat. Here is an example, later cited in the New Testament: *Rejoice greatly, O daughter Zion! Shout aloud, O daughter Jerusalem! Lo, your king comes to you; triumphant and victorious is he, humble and riding on a donkey, on a colt, the foal of a donkey* (Zechariah 9:9; see Matthew 21:5; John 12:15).

This refers to a future restoration and the joy that it will bring. The beginnings of such a positive note are found already in Isaiah 52: *Shake yourself from the dust, rise up, O captive Jerusalem; loose the bonds from your neck, O captive daughter Zion!* (Isaiah 52:2).

(ii) Marriage symbolism for God's faithfulness to Israel. At this stage, all of Isaiah 62 should really be read.

(iii) Redeemed of the Lord: in using this expression, Third Isaiah picks up a major theme of Deutero-Isaiah 40–55 (Isaiah 43:1; 44:22–23; 48:20; 52:9). For Second Isaiah, this redemption had already begun in the exile and is to be completed by the return of the deportees. God is also called a redeemer in these passages: Isaiah 41:14; 43:14; 44:6; 47:4; 48:17; 49:7, 26; 54:5, 8. In Third Isaiah, God is called redeemer three times (Isaiah 59:20; 60:16; 63:16).

Brief commentary

(V.11)
The word used for proclaim means to cause to hear (cf. the *Shema Yisrael*) and is found frequent in Isaiah 40–66 (Isaiah 41:22, 26; 42:2, 9; 43:9, 12; 44:8; 45:21; 48:3, 5–6, 20; 52:7; 58:4; 62:11). This proclamation is to the whole world – a little exaggeration in the context – but not untypical of Isaiah 40–66 (Isaiah 42:10; 43:6; 48:20; 49:6; 62:11). Recompense is a positive statement of the earlier expression: 'Speak tenderly to Jerusalem, and cry to her that she has served her term, that her penalty is paid, that she has received from the LORD's hand double for all her sins' (Isaiah 40:2).

(V. 12)
The Holy People: the force of this 'title' becomes apparent when one reads Leviticus 17–26, the so-called Holiness Code. In that portion of the book, Israel is repeatedly called to be holy as YHWH is holy (for example, Leviticus 19:2; 20:7–8, 26; 21:8, 23; 22:9, 16, 33). This

holiness of the people challenges another tradition that would confine holiness to the sanctuary. In this view, the holiness of the people is achieved through both ritual and social practices. One text may serve to illustrate: 'Consecrate yourselves therefore, and be holy; for I am the Lord your God. Keep my statutes, and observe them; I am the Lord; I sanctify you' (Leviticus 20:7–8). Remote as Leviticus may seem, it is part of the foundation of the Second Vatican Council's teaching on the Church as the people of God. The import of 'sought out' can best be felt by reading Song of Songs 3:1–2, 5:5. The other metaphors – redeemed and not forsaken – were explored a little above. It becomes evident that this apparently slight reading is full of resonance and is really very appropriate for the feast of Christmas.

Pointers for prayer

a) 'Salvation' is one of those words we use in Church circles. It might be useful to go back to any experience of your own where you felt 'saved'. Examples could be coming through a health crisis, restoring a fractured relationship, emerging from bereavement or depression. These experiences can lead to an understanding of salvation in Christ: freedom from fear of death, purpose in life, forgiveness of sins.

b) When we reflect on the Church, it is good to be reminded that it is first and foremost the people of God, even 'the holy people' of God. Through these difficult times, there is great life and hope in the continued fidelity and extraordinary commitment of the 'ordinary' faithful. Time for prayer of praise and thanks!

Prayer

Loving shepherd of the sheep, always seeking the lost and strayed, today let us hear again your good news of salvation; touch our hearts that we may know afresh your love for us in Jesus Christ, your Son, who lives and reigns with you in the unity of the Holy Spirit, in the splendour of eternal light. God for ever and ever. Amen.

Themes across the readings

The dawn Mass (perhaps rarely celebrated) has much shorter readings very suitable for the time of day: light, kindness, love, astonishment, contemplation, thanksgiving.

Chapter 8

Christmas Day: Day Mass (ABC)

Thought for the day

There is ongoing research into how certain animals manage to communicate, establishing some commonality with human beings. Such investigation makes it clear, however, that language, in its complexity and depth, is distinctively human, a mark of who we are. When we speak, something deeply personal goes out from us, in a manner of speaking. Words are personal, mysterious, powerful (cf. *a soft tongue can break a bone* from Proverbs 25:15). God, too, discloses himself: in the 'word' of creation, in the words of the prophets and, now, in the Word made flesh, God's deepest and most personal disclosure. We give thanks for God's 'eloquence' in Jesus of Nazareth, as we mark his birth.

Prayer

You have spoken, O God, shattered our deafness, and we can hear you in one like ourselves. Let us celebrate the feast, then, in love and great joy. Through Christ our Lord. Amen.

Gospel

Jn 1:1 In the beginning was the Word, and the Word was with God, and the Word was God. [2] He was in the beginning with God. [3] All things came into being through him, and without him not one thing came into being. What has come into being [4] in him was life, and the life was the light of all people. [5] The light shines in the darkness, and the darkness did not overcome it.

⁶ There was a man sent from God, whose name was John. ⁷ He came as a witness to testify to the light, so that all might believe through him. ⁸ He himself was not the light, but he came to testify to the light. ⁹ The true light, which enlightens everyone, was coming into the world.

¹⁰ He was in the world, and the world came into being through him; yet the world did not know him. ¹¹ He came to what was his own, and his own people did not accept him. ¹² But to all who received him, who believed in his name, he gave power to become children of God, ¹³ who were born, not of blood or of the will of the flesh or of the will of man, but of God.

¹⁴ And the Word became flesh and lived among us, and we have seen his glory, the glory as of a father's only son, full of grace and truth. ¹⁵ (John testified to him and cried out, 'This was he of whom I said, "He who comes after me ranks ahead of me because he was before me."') ¹⁶ From his fullness we have all received, grace upon grace. ¹⁷ The law indeed was given through Moses; grace and truth came through Jesus Christ. ¹⁸ No one has ever seen God. It is God the only Son, who is close to the Father's heart, who has made him known.

Initial observations

All four gospels open with a key to understanding Jesus' deep identity before the story of the ministry proper begins. Even Mark 1:1 fulfils this function: *the beginning of the good news of Jesus Christ, the Son of God.* The writer of the Fourth Gospel takes up the challenge of the word 'beginning' and fills it with deeper meaning for all those born again.

Kind of writing

These verses adapt an early Jewish-Christian hymn to Wisdom, which may have looked something like this:

1 In the beginning was Wisdom
and Wisdom was with God
and God (divine) was Wisdom [read: Wisdom was divine]
2 The same (she) was in the beginning with God
3a All things through her became
4 What became in her was life
And the life was the light of men
5 And the light in the darkness shines
And the darkness did not extinguish it
10 In the world she was
and the world through her became
And the world did not know her.
11 Unto her own she came,
And her own did not receive her
12a But as many as received her,
12b She gave them authority
children of God to become
14a/b And Wisdom tabernacled among us

It is likely that the final editor (i) changed the language from 'wisdom' to 'word', and (ii) inserted the prose additions putting John the Baptist firmly in his theological place (thus interrupting the poetry). (iii) Before that again, someone added elements in vv. 16–18 that have a Pauline feel to them. So, there is quite a bit of history behind the present text. The change from wisdom to word entailed the loss of the feminine imagery, alas. It brought with it the advantage that *logos* serves to unite important themes: creation (by word), prophecy (word), gospel (the word) and incarnation in the person of Jesus (the word made flesh). It mirrors the shift from Jesus in his words proclaiming the kingdom to the early Christians proclaiming Jesus as the Word and as king, God's revelation in a human person.

Scholars have also found a concentric pattern across this carefully constructed text. D gives the benefits of faith in the Word made flesh.

A. (1–5) God, creation, humans
   B. (6–8) John the Baptist

C. (9–11) The light; his rejection
D. (12–13) Faith in the Word
C'. (14) The word; his rejection
B'. (15) John the Baptist
A'. (16–18) God, creation, humans.

NB: Note the error in the Jerusalem Bible version in the lectionary. In vv. 12–13, 'who *was* born' ought to read 'who *were* born'. The difference is considerable.

Old Testament background

Read Proverbs 8:22–31.

Divine wisdom had long served as one of the most important bridge concepts for a Judaism seeking to present itself intelligibly and appealingly within the context of the wider religious and philosophical thought of the time. Within Judaism itself, Wisdom (along with Spirit and Word) was one important way of speaking of God in his creative, revelatory and redemptive immanence (Proverbs, Sirach, Wisdom, Philo of Alexandria). At the same time, the language was able to negotiate the 'beyond' of God. Judaism's (later) distinctive claim was that this wisdom was now embodied in the Torah (Sirach 24:23; Baruch 4:1). The language of 'word' (*logos*) was used by the Stoic philosophers to express the presence of God penetrating all that is (cf. Acts 17). Both the Hebrew and the Greek traditions were negotiating, so to speak, the transcendence and the immanence of God. Good examples of this kind of writing can be found in Proverbs 8 and Wisdom 7. Genesis 1:1–2:4a is also very much in the mind of the writer.

New Testament foreground

Here we notice in bullet point form the resonance of this language throughout the Fourth Gospel:
* *New creation* across the Fourth Gospel – beginning, finished, first day of the week (John 1; 20; 21). Cf. Genesis 1:1–2:4a.

- *Life* – the Lazarus story – I am the Resurrection and the Life (John 11).

- *Light* – the Blind Man – I am the Light of the world (John 9).

- *The Baptist* – important early on in the gospel (John 1–3).

- *Not know him* – the rejection by most Jews (John 5 and 18–19).

- *Children and being born* – Nicodemus (John 3).

- *Flesh* – cf. Thomas and Tiberias (John 20–21).

- *Glory* – throughout this gospel, glory and glorification are used to refer to the revelation of God's deep self in the single event of the death and resurrection of Jesus.

- *Father's only Son* – see the long discourses in John 13–17 which express and 'unpack' the relationship.

- *Truth* – Pilate and often elsewhere; I am the truth (John 19).

- *'He was before me'* – 'Before Abraham was, I Am' (John 8:58 – but throughout in the well-known I am pronouncements in this gospel).

- *Made him known* – revealed through actions and speech, seen especially in the long meditations in the Fourth Gospel (most likely not the words of the historical Jesus, but late first-century meditations).

St Paul

> For God, who said 'Let light shine out of darkness', is the one who shined in our hearts to give us the light of the glorious knowledge of God in the face of Christ. (2 Corinthians 4:6)

Brief commentary

(V. 1)
The context is the original creation and the new creation in Christ. The Word expresses and articulates the deep being of God.

(V. 2)
The New Testament writers became aware quite early of Jesus' identity with God. This is one of the strongest statements.

(V. 3)
Something similar is said in Colossians 1:15–20 and Ephesians 1:3–14.

(V. 4)
The images of light and life recur powerfully throughout this gospel.

(V. 5)
The writer states the victory of Jesus over death before coming to the tragic rejection of the Word by God's first chosen people.

(Vv. 6–9)
Anxiety about John makes the writer clarify the relationship with Jesus. This is most likely on account of the continued existence of disciples of John the Baptist, who might claim a certain superiority. Cf. Mandaeans of today.

(Vv. 10–11)
The message is both paradoxical and tragic.

(Vv. 12–13)
The literary and theological anticipation of the effects of incarnation may be seen here.

(V. 14)
An echo of both wisdom and God's presence (*shekinah*) in the ark of the covenant; at the time, highly paradoxical because of the juxtaposition of word (*logos*) and flesh (*sarx*). 'Grace and truth' are the same as 'love and faithfulness', God's covenant qualities in the Old Testament, coming to personal expression in the person of Jesus of Nazareth.

(V.15)

Here we have another prose interruption to 'locate' John the Baptist.

(V. 16)

We may speak of God's prodigal gift of love in the Son.

(V.17)

The contrast of Law and grace sounds Pauline at this point.

(V. 18)

Cf. 1 John 4:12. 'Made him known' = lit. to relate in detail, to expound or, perhaps, to tell the story.

Pointers for prayer

a) 'In the beginning' takes me back to my own new creation in Christ – back to significant moments – perhaps even to a single moment which stands out as the beginning of my own belonging in Christ. A prayer of praise.

b) Life – What makes me alive, taking hold of my imagination and energy? How is my life in Christ? Prayer of gratitude.

c) Light – a fabulous imagery. It may be that some particular land- or seascape stands out in my memory as having an especially beautiful light. Prayer of enlightenment.

d) The dark side of refusal and rejection – in my life I probably have said both yes and no to grace. Where am I now in my life? Prayer of pilgrimage.

e) Wisdom was God's presence – a feminine presence, because (to use biblical language), just as a man is 'incomplete' without the love and companionship of a woman, the human person needs to be complemented by God's wisdom.

f) The power of language in my experience is an entry point to appreciating the Word made flesh. What word am I hearing especially today?

Prayer

We praise you, gracious God, for the glad tidings of peace, the good news of salvation: your Word became flesh and we have seen his glory. Let the radiance of that glory enlighten the lives of those who celebrate his birth.

Reveal to all the world the light no darkness can extinguish, our Lord Jesus Christ, who lives and reigns with you in the unity of the Holy Spirit, in the splendour of eternal light, God for ever and ever. Amen.

🌿 Second Reading 🌿

Heb 1:1 Long ago God spoke to our ancestors in many and various ways by the prophets, [2] but in these last days he has spoken to us by a Son, whom he appointed heir of all things, through whom he also created the worlds. [3] He is the reflection (*apaūgasma*) of God's glory and the exact imprint (*charactēr*) of God's very being (*hypostāsis*), and he sustains all things by his powerful word. When he had made purification for sins, he sat down at the right hand of the Majesty on high, [4] having become as much superior to angels as the name he has inherited is more excellent than theirs.

[5] For to which of the angels did God ever say, 'You are my Son; today I have begotten you'? Or again, 'I will be his Father, and he will be my Son'? [6] And again, when he brings the firstborn into the world, he says, 'Let all God's angels worship him.'

Initial observations

The stately opening of Hebrews, sonorous even in English, makes this an ideal reading for Christmas day – poetic and dignified, mysterious and intriguing. Even here, however, something of the puzzle of Hebrews come to the fore. Who wrote it? To whom? When? In what circumstances? Much remains speculative, although the implied context can be inferred (see next section). Today, scholars would claim this is not a letter but a homily in which the author wants to show that Jesus' death *both* fulfils *and* abolishes the Temple service. This deep understanding of Jesus' death and resurrection is built upon the foundation of Jesus as the final and complete disclosure of God (Son, heir, 'reflection' and 'imprint').

Kind of writing

This early Christian homily is written in the best Greek of the New Testament, using all the techniques of ancient rhetoric, 'the art of speaking well'. In particular, we note the sustained use of comparison (*synkrisis*): prophets, angels, Moses, Aaron and the Temple cult. Our reading is part of the introduction to the opening section, Hebrews 1:1–4; 1:5–4:13. The four opening verses form an introduction (*exordium*), while vv. 5–6 initiate the first comparison with the angels. As an *exordium*, the opening verses attract the attention and good will of the audience and lay out the themes to be treated in the course of the whole homily.

Origin of the reading

A careful reading of the letter allows a tentative reconstruction of the context of writing. (i) The community, after initial conversion and enthusiasm, encountered considerable opposition from the surrounding culture. (ii) Within the group, some fell away because of the gap between Christian claims and reality. (iii) The many exhortations reveal the anxiety of the author that more will fall away. (iv) The teaching that 'Jesus can help us because he is like us' reveals the context of suffering and trials and a sense of alienation. The author addresses the context in two ways: theology (really Christology) and much practical exhortation/ *paraenesis*. Our verses focus on the Christology of Hebrews.

Related passages

Many New Testament passages echo the high Christology of Hebrews.

- All things came into being through him, and without him not one thing came into being. (John 1:3)

- For from him and through him and to him are all things. To him be the glory forever. Amen. (Romans 11:36)

- Indeed, even though there may be so-called gods in heaven or on earth – as in fact there are many gods and many lords – yet for us there is one God, the Father, from whom are all things and for whom we exist, and one Lord, Jesus Christ, through whom are all things and through whom we exist. (1 Corinthians 8:5–6)

- He is the image of the invisible God, the firstborn of all creation; for in him all things in heaven and on earth were created, things visible and invisible, whether thrones or dominions or rulers or powers – all things have been created through him and for him. (Colossians 1:15–16)

- For it is the God who said, 'Let light shine out of darkness', who has shone in our hearts to give the light of the knowledge of the glory of God in the face of Jesus Christ. (2 Corinthians 4:6)

Brief commentary

(V. 1)
Already the tone of comparison is established, within an affirmation of continuity (*our* ancestors ... *but*).

(V. 2)
Notice how comprehensive the claims are: the present (Son), the end/future (heir), the beginning/past (creation). As believers, we become accustomed to such claims but, as Raymond Brown remarked many years ago, these *are* extraordinary claims about a Galilean peasant prophet who was put to death ignominiously by the Romans.

(V. 3a)
The imagery here (given in Greek above) comes not only from the Wisdom tradition of the Bible but also from philosophical speculation, in the works of Philo of Alexandria, for example.

(V. 3b)

Thus the writer announces the main argument of Hebrews: Jesus fulfils, transcends and abolishes the Temple priesthood. The challenge is acute because the *historical* Jesus was a prophet and a layman, not a priest.

(V. 4)

The final sentence of the introduction acts as a bridge to the next section, the comparison with the angels.

(V. 5)

The rhetorical questions make use of Psalm 2, found elsewhere (Acts 13:23; Hebrews 5:5). At the time, Psalm 2 was widely read in a messianic manner.

(V. 6)

The verse cited is from the Septuagint of Deuteronomy 32:43: *Be glad, O nations, with his people, and let all the angels of God prevail* (= *worship* in Hebrews) *for him.*

Pointers for prayer

a) Can I go back to my own times of 'disclosure', when I was aware of God's word to me in a special way?

b) Christians don't just say things *about* Jesus; instead, we encounter him as God's living word in our world. Building on such personal experience, we become more and more aware of the depth and mystery of the identity of Jesus.

Prayer

In your words to us, O God, you have disclosed yourself and guided our steps. In the Word made flesh, you have done something even more wonderful: we see the very imprint of your being, as you speak to us from within our fractured humanity. Help us to come to you through Jesus, our Lord and brother who can help us because he is one of us and knows our lives from the inside out. Through Christ our Lord. Amen.

🌿 First Reading 🌿

Is 52:7   How delightful it is to see approaching over the mountains
the feet of a messenger who announces peace,
a messenger who brings good news, who announces deliverance,
who says to Zion, 'Your God reigns!'

8   Listen, your watchmen shout;
in unison they shout for joy,
for they see with their very own eyes
the LORD's return to Zion.

9   In unison give a joyful shout,
O ruins of Jerusalem!
For the LORD consoles his people;
he protects Jerusalem.

10   The LORD reveals his royal power
in the sight of all the nations;
the entire earth sees
our God deliver.

Initial observations

This reading is very suitable for the third mass of Christmas Day. It
has an energetic, uplifting tone and the words touch on the important
themes of the feast (peace, good news, salvation, joy and so forth).

Kind of writing

Once again, this is poetry, showing the usual marks of parallelism. Part
of the imagery includes reference to the Holy City (Zion, Jerusalem,
sentinels on the look-out). We see also the language of proclamation
(announces, brings good news), the language of response (sing, joy,
singing), and the language of God's gifts (peace, good news, salvation,
return, comforted, redeemed, holy arm, salvation of our God). The
pleasure of biblical parallelism can be noted here:

> 7 who brings good news,
> who announces salvation,
> who says to Zion, 'Your God reigns.'

⁸ Listen! Your sentinels lift up their voices,
together they sing for joy;
⁹ for the Lord has comforted his people,
he has redeemed Jerusalem.

It is said once more that God will be returning with them, because in Exile God was with them all along. It shares that vision with Isaiah 40:3–5 (see below). It may well be that the exhilaration found here comes from some who returned early and felt the relief and joy.

Origin of the reading

As we have seen regularly in Advent, Isaiah is almost a fifth gospel for early Christianity, so widely was it used. It does come from a difficult time, that is, during the Babylonian Exile (587–539 BC). The whole section runs from our v. 7 as far as v.12. It is, in effect, a prophecy of restoration, offering the exiles an ecstatic vision of hope and renewal. It comes as a response to v. 6 just before, which reads: *Therefore my people shall know my name; therefore in that day they shall know that it is I who speak; here am* (Isaiah 52:6).

Related passages

A voice cries out: 'In the wilderness prepare the way of the LORD, make straight in the desert a highway for our God. Every valley shall be lifted up, and every mountain and hill be made low; the uneven ground shall become level, and the rough places a plain. Then the glory of the LORD shall be revealed, and all people shall see it together, for the mouth of the LORD has spoken.' (Isaiah 40:3–5)

Then the watcher called out: 'Upon a watchtower I stand, O LORD, continually by day, and at my post I am stationed throughout the night. (Isaiah 21:8)

Lift up your heads, O gates! and be lifted up, O ancient doors! that the King of glory may come in. Who is the King of glory? The LORD, strong and mighty, the LORD, mighty in battle. Lift up your heads, O gates! and be lifted up, O ancient doors! that the King of glory may come in. Who is this King of glory? The LORD of hosts, he is the King of glory. (Psalm 24:7–10). Cf. Psalm 47:1–9.

Brief commentary

(V. 7)
In a striking rhetorical figure, even the (presumably humble, even pedestrian!) feet of the messengers are praised for their beauty! The message is peace, *shalom*, i.e. a gift of wholeness, affecting the whole person within a network of relationships. It includes the healing of wound of the Exile for one and for all.

The imagery echoes that of a victorious monarch returning. 'Bringing good news' is a verb in the Hebrew Bible ('goodnewsing', or something like that – in any case an action). The New Testament noun gospel or good news comes precisely from Isaiah. The psalms often speak of universal salvation (Psalm 96:10; 97:1; 99:1).

(V. 8)
This verse voices the longing of those in the city who are on the alert for God's return. There is a contrast with Isaiah 21:8, where one sentinel is alone. Here, they are united in their reaction to the 'second exodus' of God's return to Zion.

(V. 9)
This captures the context of the Exile – the ruin of Jerusalem. God comforts by means of redemption or salvation. Poetically, it is the very stones of Jerusalem that cry out.

(V. 10)
The arm is a standard image in the Bible for the power of God and to bare the arm is to let God's power be seen or felt. In the eyes of the poet, this is an international event, taking place in sight of all the nations, all the ends of the earth. See Psalm 98.

Pointers for prayer

a) To hear good news is a wonderful thing. Go back to some experience of your own which brought you particular delight. When did you first come to appreciate the good news of the kingdom of God?

b) Peace is also a wonderful word, particularly in the Bible, where it means health, prosperity, good relationships. Thank God for the well-being you enjoy!

c) The joy that Christmas brings comes to delightful expression in today's first reading. Let the happiness of the feast touch your own heart today, so that you are renewed in Christ and have cause for singing.

d) Salvation for all is the great message of Christmas: This is our God and we extol him. *No one has ever seen God. It is God the only Son, who is close to the Father's heart, who has made him known* (John 1:18). Let us rejoice and be glad!

Prayer

God, so close to us that we can hardly believe it, draw us into the circle of your love so that our celebration of the birth of Christ will bring us new life and true joy as we continue on the way of your salvation. Through Christ our Lord. Amen.

Themes across the readings

The readings for the day Mass invite us to lift of our sights: the birth of Jesus *matters* for all humanity, for the world as a whole and even for the cosmos. In him, creation comes to fulfilment and in him creation itself is made new. It is a grand vision – yet rooted in history, in the individual, concrete life of Jesus of Nazareth. 'Indeed, from his fullness we have, all of us, received.'

Chapter 9

Holy Family C

Thought for the day

Today we have a chance to reflect on the *mystery* of our own families! It really *is* a bit of mystery, how we mostly come out okay from this most intense and formative of experiences. We receive so much that we really want to ponder and to treasure. We can also be burdened by attitudes and traits that we might well wish we were without. Yet, through it all, we are grateful. Family is our 'first love' and never really loses its importance for us.

Prayer

Bless all our families. We thank you for the very gift of life itself we have through our parents and for all the other many gifts we receive from our families. We have received so much: help us to continue to give. Help us too to know what to overlook and forget, to pay attention to what can be healed and forgiven, and through it all to continue to love. Through Christ our Lord. Amen.

Gospel

Lk 2:41 Now every year the parents of Jesus went to Jerusalem for the festival of the Passover. [42] And when he was twelve years old, they went up as usual for the festival. [43] When the festival was ended and they started to return, the boy Jesus stayed behind in Jerusalem, but his parents did not know it. [44] Assuming that he was in the group of travellers, they went a day's journey. Then they started to look for him among their relatives and friends. ⁴⁵ When they did not find him, they returned to Jerusalem to search for him. ⁴⁶ After three days they found him in the temple, sitting among the teachers, listening to them and asking them questions. ⁴⁷ And all who heard him were amazed at his understanding and his answers. ⁴⁸ When his parents saw him they were astonished; and his mother said to him, 'Child, why have you treated us like this? Look, your father and I have been searching for you in great anxiety.' ⁴⁹ He said to them, 'Why were you searching for me? Did you not know that I must be in my Father's house?' ⁵⁰ But they did not understand what he said to them. ⁵¹ Then he went down with them and came to Nazareth, and was obedient to them. His mother treasured all these things in her heart.

⁵² And Jesus increased in wisdom and in years, and in divine and human favour.

Initial observations

Jesus in the Temple is a story unique to Luke's Gospel. Luke may well be using a source here (there seems to be no awareness of the virginal conception in the story). Rather than an innocent reminiscence, the story bears the marks of post-Easter composition.

This deceptively simple tale serves several purposes of the evangelist. (i) It reminds us of the Jewishness of Jesus and his family. (ii) It fulfils one of the conventions of ancient biography: childhood prodigies. (iii) It begins the portrait of Jesus as a prophet and as a reader of Scripture. (iv) It portrays Jesus as a human being, experiencing the ordinary development from childhood onwards. (v) It shows Jesus himself taking 'ownership' of all the things said of him thus far in the Infancy Narrative of Luke.

All five elements are significant for Luke. He is very likely writing against what we may call proto-Marcionism, the desire to uproot Jesus from his Jewish matrix, and behind that a desire to dismiss Judaism as somehow surpassed and superseded. He may also be countering the beginnings of Apollinarianism, evident in other non-canonical accounts of Jesus' childhood. Typically, these so emphasise the divinity of the child Jesus that he seems hardly human. There is a considerable contrast, for example, with the *Infancy Gospel of Thomas* (quoted below; you can find it here: www.gnosis.org).

Kind of writing

Typically, biography of the period included these elements: pre-public career of a great person, family background, miraculous conception, omens and other predictions of future greatness, childhood prodigies. These are found in Greek, Roman and Jewish documents of the period: e.g. Cyrus (*Herodotus* I, 114f.), Alexander the Great (Plutarch, *Life of Alexander* 5), Moses (Josephus, *Antiquities* 2:230; Philo, *Life of Moses* 1.21). All these elements are registered in Luke 1–2.

One example may suffice. Josephus, the Jewish priest and historian, untrammelled by false modesty, says of himself:

'When I was a child, about fourteen years of age, I was commended by all for the love I had of learning; on which account the high priests and principal men of the city frequently came to me together, to know my opinion about the accurate understanding of points of the law.' (Josephus, *Life* 9)

Two observations may help us grasp more clearly the purpose of the story. Firstly, it does show a concentric pattern as follows:

A The family goes to Jerusalem (41–42)
  B Jesus remains, unobserved (43)
    C The parents' search (44–46a)
      D *Jesus among the teachers* (46b–47)
    C* The parents' reproach (48)
  B* Jesus replies, misunderstood (49–50)
A* The family returns to Nazareth (51a)

In such a layout, the focus falls on Jesus as source of wisdom, a characterisation that will continue through the gospel as Jesus interprets the Scriptures on his own authority (Luke 4:1–13; 4:16–21; 7:26–27; 10:25–28; 20:17–18; 20:37–38; 20:41–44; 24:25–27, 32; 24:44–47).

Secondly, the climax in terms of plot must fall on B*, when Jesus makes his transparently enigmatic response. The complication in v. 43 leads to this climax in the form of dialogue and thus the emphasis really falls on the *future career* of the child prodigy.

Old Testament background

> Three times in the year you shall hold a festival for me. You shall observe the festival of unleavened bread; as I commanded you, you shall eat unleavened bread for seven days at the appointed time in the month of Abib, for in it you came out of Egypt. No one shall appear before me empty-handed. You shall observe the festival of harvest, of the first fruits of your labour, of what you sow in the field. You shall observe the festival of ingathering at the end of the year, when you gather in from the field the fruit of your labour. Three times in the year all your males shall appear before the Lord God. (Exodus 23:14–17)

Cf. also Deuteronomy 16:1–8,16–17 and Luke 22:7–13.

> Now the boy Samuel continued to grow both in stature and in favour with the Lord and with the people. (1 Samuel 2:26)

New Testament foreground

> Therefore he had to become like his brothers and sisters in every respect, so that he might be a merciful and faithful high priest in the service of God, to make a sacrifice of atonement for the sins of the people. (Hebrews 2:17)

> For we do not have a high priest who is unable to sympathise with our weaknesses, but we have one who in every respect has been tested as we are, yet without sin. (Hebrews 4:15)

St Paul

> But when the appropriate time had come, God sent out his Son, born of a woman, born under the law, to redeem those who were under the law, so that we may be adopted as sons with full rights. And because you are sons, God sent the Spirit of his Son into our hearts, who calls 'Abba! Father!' So you are no longer a slave but a son, and if you are a son, then you are also an heir through God. (Galatians 4:4–7)

Brief commentary

(V. 41)
The scene is set with characters, time and place. As often in the introduction, we are told *what they usually did.* This tells us that they are an observant, pious family.

(V. 42)
In Israelite tradition, one passed from childhood to adulthood at the age of thirteen (teenagers had not yet been invented). Accordingly, Jesus is still a child. The association with *Bar Mitzvah* seems to be out of place. The 'as usual' is a hint of things to come: Jesus is shown regularly praying and going to the synagogue 'as was his custom'.

(V. 43)
The details arouses our interest: How did this happen, when will the parents notice, what will they do? Above all, what will be the outcome?

(V. 44)
The reaction adds suspense by slowing down the telling.

(V. 45)
The suspense is sustained. In this gospel, Jerusalem functions as the *location* of salvation. Towards the end of the gospel, there will be another return to Jerusalem: That same hour they got up and returned to Jerusalem. (Luke 24:33)

(V.46)

In popular stories, the number three is important but here it must have a resonance for the reader familiar with the Jesus story.

(V. 47)

Cf. the reaction of one expert in the *Infancy Gospel of Thomas*, chapter 7:

> *Now when Zacchaeus the teacher heard such and so many allegories of the first letter spoken by the young child, he was perplexed at his answer and his instruction being so great, and said to them that were there: Woe is me, wretch that I am, I am confounded: I have brought shame to myself by drawing to me this young child. Take him away, therefore I beseech thee, my brother Joseph: I cannot endure the severity of his look, I cannot once make clear my (or his) word. This young child is not earthly born: this is one that can tame even fire: be like this is one begotten before the making of the world. ... I have deceived myself, thrice wretched man that I am: I strove to get me a disciple and I am found to have a master.*

(V. 48)

This is the emotional climax of the story. To express the anxiety of the parents, the narrative at last breaks into dialogue.

(V. 49)

There are two possible translations here, because the Greek does not contain the word 'house'. Instead, it runs literally, *I must be 'in the things' of my father*. So we can translate by Temple, my father's house, although the usage is unusual. It may also be rendered 'my father's business', as in the Douai-Rheims translation (also the King James Bible and the Jerusalem Bible).

The 'must' is part of the 'divine imperative' found elsewhere in the narrative: Luke 4:43; 9:22; 11:42; 17:25; 22:37.

(V. 51)

A double conclusion, showing Jesus to be fully human and taking up once more the pondering of Mary.

(V. 52)

An inclusion: *The child grew and became strong, filled with wisdom; and the favour of God was upon him* (Luke 2:40). Cf. *The child grew and became strong in spirit, and he was in the wilderness until the day he appeared publicly to Israel* (Luke 1:80).

Pointers for prayer

a) Luke's skill as a story-teller comes through in the details of the story in a way that many people can identify with: the losing of a child, the frantic search, the seemingly offhand speech of the boy. Let the drama of the story speak to you. Where do you find good news in it?

b) In Luke's Gospel this story serves to give a glimpse of the future greatness of Jesus, the teacher of his people. Sometimes we can look back over our own life, or the lives of others, and with hindsight can see in childhood or teenage years a glimpse of gifts and talents that were later to blossom. Where have you seen this?

c) 'Did you not know that I must be about my Father's business?' This seemingly insensitive reply by Jesus to Mary serves to highlight that in his life the mission given him by God would take precedence over family ties, painful though this would be. Perhaps you have known situations in your own life, or in the life of another, where there was pain for family members as you followed your own destiny? Where in the midst of the pain was the good news?

Prayer

As your sons and daughters, O loving God, we come before you in thanksgiving, called and united by your eternal Word.

Teach us to ponder the mystery of Nazareth, that we may always find in you the source of our strength and the unity of our families.

We ask this through Jesus Christ, your Word made flesh, who lives and reigns with you in the unity of the Holy Spirit, in the splendour of eternal light, God for ever and ever. Amen.

⚘ Second reading ⚘

1 Jn 3:1 See what love the Father has given us, that we should be called children of God; and that is what we are. The reason the world does not know us is that it did not know him. **²** Beloved, we are God's children now; what we will be has not yet been revealed. What we do know is this: when he is revealed, we will be like him, for we will see him as he is. **³** *And all who have this hope in him purify themselves, just as he is pure.*

²³ And this is his commandment, that we should believe in the name of his Son Jesus Christ and love one another, just as he has commanded us. **²⁴** All who obey his commandments abide in him, and he abides in them. And by this we know that he abides in us, by the Spirit that he has given us.

Initial observations

The reading helpfully shifts the focus of the feast to the family *of the faith*. The author wants to remind us deeply and richly of our being children of God. He knows well that this 'being born again' is mysterious in the present, not to speak of into the future.

Kind of writing

The whole document – more of a sermon than a letter and perhaps a hybrid category, epistolary sermon – does it justice. To deepen his teaching, the author relies upon a circular, repetitive style, wherein the same material is revisited in another light.

| 1:1–4 | Introduction |
| 1:5–2:17 | Exhortation |

Accordingly, our reading should be read in light of the whole section 2:28–3:24.

Origin of the reading

The content is appropriate at any time in Christian reflection. Perhaps, however, it was even more appropriate to those who first read the Fourth Gospel, which had, it would seem, been both understood and misunderstood.

We know already from that gospel that some kind of break has taken place, precisely over the identity of Jesus: *When many of his disciples heard it, they said, 'This teaching is difficult; who can accept it?' Because of this many of his disciples turned back and no longer went about with him* (John 6:60, 66).

Related passages

> Beloved, let us love one another, because love is from God; everyone who loves is born of God and knows God. Whoever does not love does not know God, for God is love. God's love was revealed among us in this way: God sent his only Son into the world so that we might live through him. In this is love, not that we loved God but that he loved us and sent his Son to be the atoning sacrifice for our sins. Beloved, since God loved us so much, we also ought to love one another. No one has ever seen God; if we love one another, God lives in us, and his love is perfected in us. (1 John 4:7–12)

> So we have known and believe the love that God has for us. God is love, and those who abide in love abide in God, and

God abides in them. (1 John 4:16)

Everyone who believes that Jesus is the Christ has been born of God, and everyone who loves the parent loves the child. (1 John 5:1)

But to all who received him, who believed in his name, he gave power to become children of God, who were born, not of blood or of the will of the flesh or of the will of man, but of God. (John 1:12–13)

Brief commentary

(V. 1)

A new exhortation starts with the imperative 'See'. This writer reserves the expression 'son of God' (*huios tou theou*) for Jesus and uses instead 'children of God' (*tekna theou*) for believers. This gift is a measure of God's love, a love directed to the future. The community may feel not recognised, but the writer explains why. It's nothing to do with them (or us): the 'world' does not know God *and therefore* does not know those who believe in God.

(V. 2)

The favourite address 'beloved' underscores the love of God from the previous verse. Our whole goal is to be 'like' God – a breathtaking goal. It does mean that our present reality, however rich and deep, does not exhaust what God has in store. This is a rare eschatological view in the Johannine texts. Something beyond what we could know or even imagine is offered. Cf. Jesus answered him, 'Very truly, I tell you, no one can see the kingdom of God without being born from above' (John 3:3). (1 John 3:3, essential from the writer's viewpoint, is omitted in the lectionary.)

(V. 23)

This section is coming to a close and a concluding summary is being offered. *We* tend to summarise the gospel as love of God and neighbour (not inaccurately and indeed on the basis of Jesus' teaching). However, our author has another perspective: first Christ and then the practice of love. *And this is eternal life, that they may know you, the only true God, and Jesus Christ whom you have sent* (John 17:3).*But these are written so that you may come to believe that Jesus is the Messiah, the Son of God, and that through believing you may have life in his name* (John 20:31).

It parallels his teaching on the love of God: God loved us first. Our faith and our love are not without doctrinal content. At the same time, the vertical is matched by the earnest horizontal of practical love and service. For all the talk of love, commandments are huge in the letters of John: 1 John 2:3–4, 7–8; 3:22–24; 4:21; 5:2–3; 2 John 1:5–6 (cf. in the gospel: John 12:49–50; 13:34; 14:15, 21; 15:10, 12).

(V. 24)

Our 'being in God' is finally looked at from two perspectives, both familiar from the Fourth Gospel. *If you keep my commandments, you will abide in my love, just as I have kept my Father's commandments and abide in his love* (John 15:10).*What is born of the flesh is flesh, and what is born of the Spirit is spirit* (John 3:6).*When he had said this, he breathed on them and said to them, 'Receive the Holy Spirit'* (John 20:22).

Pointers for prayer

a) Christmas is *our* birth as well: let us celebrate and rejoice and give thanks.

b) Eternal life is surely abstract but believing in Christ and loving our neighbour are not: on the contrary!

c) The writer affirms the presence and the action of the Spirit in the lives of believers. How do I listen to the inspiration of the Spirit in my life as a disciple?

Prayer

Father, let your love penetrate our hearts; help us, your children, to live the love we have received in Jesus. Through the same Christ, our Lord. Amen.

🌿 First reading 🌿

1 Sam 1:20 In due time Hannah conceived and bore a son. She named him Samuel, for she said, 'I have asked (*šeʾiltîw*) him of the LORD.'

²¹ The man Elkanah and all his household went up to offer to the LORD the yearly sacrifice, and to pay his vow. ²² But Hannah did not go up, for she said to her husband, 'As soon as the child is weaned, I will bring him, that he may appear in the presence of the LORD, and remain there forever; I will offer him as a nazirite for all time.' ²³ *Her husband Elkanah said to her, 'Do what seems best to you, wait until you have weaned him; only – may the* LORD *establish his word.' So the woman remained and nursed her son, until she weaned him.* ²⁴ When she had weaned him, she took him up with her, along with a three-year-old bull, an ephah of flour, and a skin of wine. She brought him to the house of the LORD at Shiloh; and the child was young. ²⁵ Then they slaughtered the bull, and they brought the child to Eli. ²⁶ And she said, 'Oh, my LORD! As you live, my LORD, I am the woman who was standing here in your presence, praying to the LORD. ²⁷ For this child I prayed; and the LORD has granted me the petition that I made (*šeʾēlātî*) to him. ²⁸ Therefore I have lent (*hišʾiltihû*) him to the LORD; as long as he lives, he is given (*šāʾûl*) to the LORD.' She left him there for the LORD.

Initial observations

This is the chosen reading for Year C. Nevertheless, it is a little unusual, given that it tells the story of a mother who, having given birth to the longed-for child, now hands him over to service in the Temple at the very young age of about three years. Not an example many parents would be inclined to follow! The essential and very touching context is given in the related passages below.

Kind of writing

The preceding story of promise resembles other annunciation stories and Hannah's prayer is very like the individual psalms of distress. As we take up the story, YHWH has 'remembered' Hannah and she gives birth to a son. The purpose of this intricate story of conception and birth is to underline the divine intervention in the birth of Samuel and the family context of both disdain (from the other wife) and devotion (from her husband).

Origin of the reading

1 Samuel begins with an account of the birth of the prophet. The story illustrates the motif of the 'barren matriarch' whose child will somehow be significant in the story of salvation. For example, Sarah, Rachel, the wife of Minoah and mother of Samson. Frequently, this is interlaced with domestic friction with another wife/sister who is fertile. Analysis of 1–2 Samuel and 1–2 Kings is complex. It may be sufficient to note that 1 Samuel starts with the Song of Hannah (1 Samuel 2) and closes with the Song of David (1 Samuel 23). This *literary* frame serves also as a *theological* frame. Contrary to first impressions, the history of Israel is not all war and blood but actually the story of YHWH's salvation.

Related passages

> There was a certain man of Ramathaim, a Zuphite from the hill country of Ephraim, whose name was Elkanah son of Jeroham son of Elihu son of Tohu son of Zuph, an Ephraimite. He had two wives; the name of the one was Hannah, and the name of the other Peninnah. Peninnah had children, but Hannah had no children. Now this man used to go up year by year from his town to worship and to sacrifice to the LORD of hosts at Shiloh, where the two sons of Eli, Hophni and Phinehas, were priests of the LORD. On the day when Elkanah sacrificed, he would give portions to his wife

Peninnah and to all her sons and daughters; but to Hannah he gave a double portion, because he loved her, though the LORD had closed her womb. Her rival used to provoke her severely, to irritate her, because the LORD had closed her womb.

So it went on year by year; as often as she went up to the house of the LORD, she used to provoke her. Therefore Hannah wept and would not eat. Her husband Elkanah said to her, 'Hannah, why do you weep? Why do you not eat? Why is your heart sad? Am I not more to you than ten sons?' (1 Samuel 1:1–8; see also vv. 9–19)

Brief commentary

(V. 20)
The conception and birth are speedily dispatched. The choice of name is explained etymologically. The name may mean God (*el*) has heard (*shama*).

(V. 21)
A whole year has passed and it is time for Elkanah to officiate again at Shiloh.

(V. 22)
Hannah decides not to go up until the child is robust enough to be left there. 'Nazirites' occurs more frequently than one might imagine: Numbers 6:2, 4–5, 8, 12–13, 18–21; Judges 13:5, 7; 16:17; 1 Samuel 1:11, 22; Amos 2:11–12; 1 Maccabees 3:49. These were men and women, consecrated to God for a specific period. See Numbers 6:1–21. Matthew hints at this in his combined (and non-existent) citation *There he made his home in a town called Nazareth, so that what had been spoken through the prophets might be fulfilled, 'He will be called a Nazarene'* (Matthew 2:23) .

(V. 23)
The father agrees, adding a prayer for the future of Samuel. Weaning could take up to three years (cf. 2 Maccabees 7:27).

(V. 24)

The gifts are substantial and notably valuable. Shiloh was the chief northern shrine through much of the pre-monarchic period.

(V.25)

To understand the role of Eli, read 1 Samuel 1:9–18. Eli is no great 'discerner', as we see shortly in 1 Samuel 3.

(Vv. 26–27)

Eli had mediated the blessing and now he receives the fruit of God's intervention.

(V. 28)

Word play is meant to be instructive here (see the insertions in the text): to ask, to loan and to give all play on the consonants of *sha'al*, to ask. The child will be a 'Saul' to God. The great Song of Hannah follows, the basis for the Magnificat.

Pointers for prayer

a) This is a story of God's grace to Hannah, a story of new life from barrenness. It can be our story too.

b) This is also a story of need, trust and petition, and we may add stubbornness. Persistence in prayer means not so much spending time as coming from deep within.

Prayer

Help us, Lord, to be patient and persistent in prayer. Even before we speak, you know already what we need. We trust in the gifts you want to give us, if only we had hearts and lives to receive them. Through Christ our Lord. Amen.

Themes across the readings

In both readings, we see portrayed couples full of devotion, tenderness and faith. God did indeed establish the word of Samuel and in Jesus established his word made flesh. The centre of action in both stories is a temple, the earlier one at Shiloh and the later one in Jerusalem. Psalm 84 (83) takes up the theme of longing for the Temple, so present in both the first reading and in the gospel. The third strophe suits Hannah especially: *O Lord God of hosts, hear my prayer, give ear, O God of Jacob.*

Chapter 10

Second Sunday of Christmas C

Thought for the day

We are at the start of the new civil year. Beginning again is an invitation to look in two directions. What happened for me in the last year, both in my ordinary life and in my life as a believer, a person of faith? For what do I ask forgiveness? For what do I give thanks? We also look forward, and the new beginning gives us a chance to start again on the way of discipleship. Both thanksgiving and renewal are to be found in today's readings. The gospel is in invitation to wake up, to keep watch, to live fully the present moment under God, in whom we live and move and have our being.

Prayer

Wake us up, O God, at the start of a new year and rouse us from the slumber of the everyday that we may recognise you in every moment and in every person every day of our lives. Through Christ our Lord. Amen.

🌿 Gospel 🍃

Jn 1:1 In the beginning was the Word, and the Word was with God, and the Word was God. [2] He was in the beginning with God. [3] All things came to be through him, and without him nothing came to be. What came to be [4] through him was life, and this life was the light of the human race; [5] the light shines in the darkness, and the darkness has not overcome it. [6] A man named John was sent from God. [7] He came for testimony, to testify to the light, so that all might believe through him. [8] He was not the light, but came to testify to the light. [9] The true light, which enlightens everyone, was coming into the world.

[10] He was in the world, and the world came to be through him, but the world did not know him. [11] He came to what was his own, but his own people did not accept him. [12] But to those who did accept him he gave power to become children of God, to those who believe in his name, [13] who were born not by natural generation nor by human choice nor by a man's decision but of God.

[14] And the Word became flesh and made his dwelling among us, and we saw his glory, the glory as of the Father's only Son, full of grace and truth.

[15] John testified to him and cried out, saying, 'This was he of whom I said, "The one who is coming after me ranks ahead of me because he existed before me." [16] From his fullness we have all received, grace in place of grace, [17] because while the law was given through Moses, grace and truth came through Jesus Christ. [18] No one has ever seen God. The only Son, God, who is at the Father's side, has revealed him.

Initial observations

The Prologue was already commented on for third Mass of Christmas Day (see notes there). For today, a different translation (New American Bible Revised version) and a different commentary will be offered.

Kind of writing

Our reading is poetry – Wisdom poetry – with insistent prose interruptions.

Old Testament background

It would be a great help to look up these passages about 'Lady Wisdom': Job 28; Proverbs 1, 8, 9; Baruch 3:9–4:4; Sirach 24; Wisdom 7:7–9:18.

New Testament foreground

> We declare to you what was from the beginning, what we have heard, what we have seen with our eyes, what we have looked at and touched with our hands, concerning the word of life – this life was revealed, and we have seen it and testify to it, and declare to you the eternal life that was with the Father and was revealed to us – we declare to you what we have seen and heard so that you also may have fellowship with us; and truly our fellowship is with the Father and with his Son Jesus Christ. We are writing these things so that our joy may be complete. (1 John 1:1–4)

> Beloved, do not believe every spirit, but test the spirits to see whether they are from God; for many false prophets have gone out into the world. By this you know the Spirit of God: every spirit that confesses that Jesus Christ has come in the flesh is from God, and every spirit that does not confess Jesus is not from God. And this is the spirit of the antichrist, of which you have heard that it is coming; and now it is already in the world. Little children, you are from God, and have conquered them; for the one who is in you is greater than the one who is in the world. (1 John 4:1–4)

St Paul

> But when the appropriate time had come, God sent out his Son, born of a woman, born under the law, to redeem those who were under the law, so that we may be adopted as sons with full rights. And because you are sons, God sent the Spirit of his Son into our hearts, who calls '*Abba*! Father!' So you are

no longer a slave but a son, and if you are a son, then you are also an heir through God. (Galatians 4:4–7)

Brief commentary

The commentary takes the form of showing where the topics and images occur again throughout the Gospel according to John. In this way, the function of the Prologue as a true introduction becomes clear.

(V. 1)
New Creation: When Jesus had received the wine, he said, 'It is finished.' Then he bowed his head and gave up his spirit(John 19:30). When he had said this, he breathed on them and said to them, 'Receive the Holy Spirit' (John 20:22). Cf. John 20:1.

(V. 2)
Union with the Father: The Father and I are one (John 10:30). So now, Father, glorify me in your own presence with the glory that I had in your presence before the world existed (John 17:5).

(V. 3)
Through him: No one comes to the Father except through me (John 14:6). Indeed, God did not send the Son into the world to condemn the world, but in order that the world might be saved through him(John 3:17).

(V. 4)
Life and light: I am the way, and the truth, and the life (John 14:6). Jesus said to her, 'I am the resurrection and the life. Those who believe in me, even though they die, will live, and everyone who lives and believes in me will never die (John 11:25–26). And this is eternal life, that they may know you, the only true God, and Jesus Christ whom you have sent (John 17:3).

(V. 5)
Light and darkness: And this is the judgement, that the light has come into the world, and people loved darkness rather than light because their

deeds were evil (John 3:19). Again Jesus spoke to them, saying, 'I am the light of the world. Whoever follows me will never walk in darkness but will have the light of life' (John 8:12).

(Vv. 6–8)
John the Baptist: Cf. John 1:19–23.

(V. 9)
Into the world: When the people saw the sign that he had done, they began to say, 'This is indeed the prophet who is to come into the world' (John 6:14). She said to him, 'Yes, Lord, I believe that you are the Messiah, the Son of God, the one coming into the world' (John 11:27). Pilate asked him, 'So you are a king?' Jesus answered, 'You say that I am a king. For this I was born, and for this I came into the world, to testify to the truth. Everyone who belongs to the truth listens to my voice' (John 18:37).

(V. 10)
Did not receive him: This is the Spirit of truth, whom the world cannot receive, because it neither sees him nor knows him. You know him, because he abides with you, and he will be in you (John 14:17).

(V.11)
Opposition of his own: The man went away and told the Jews that it was Jesus who had made him well. Therefore the Jews started persecuting Jesus, because he was doing such things on the sabbath (John 5:15–17). The Jews then disputed among themselves, saying, 'How can this man give us his flesh to eat?' (John 6:52). The Jews said to him, 'Now we know that you have a demon. Abraham died, and so did the prophets; yet you say, "Whoever keeps my word will never taste death." '(John 8:52). The Jews answered, 'It is not for a good work that we are going to stone you, but for blasphemy, because you, though only a human being, are making yourself God' (John 10:33). The Jews answered him, 'We have a law, and according to that law he ought to die because he has claimed to be the Son of God' (John 19:7).

(V. 12)

Children of God: He did not say this on his own, but being high priest that year he prophesied that Jesus was about to die for the nation, and not for the nation only, but to gather into one the dispersed children of God (John 11:51–52). While you have the light, believe in the light, so that you may become children of light' (John 12:36). Cf. John 21:5.

(V. 13)

Born of God: Jesus answered him, 'Very truly, I tell you, no one can see the kingdom of God without being born from above.' Nicodemus said to him, 'How can anyone be born after having grown old? Can one enter a second time into the mother's womb and be born?' Jesus answered, 'Very truly, I tell you, no one can enter the kingdom of God without being born of water and Spirit. What is born of the flesh is flesh, and what is born of the Spirit is spirit. Do not be astonished that I said to you, 'You must be born from above.' The wind blows where it chooses, and you hear the sound of it, but you do not know where it comes from or where it goes. So it is with everyone who is born of the Spirit' (John 3:3–8). Cf. John 15:4–5.

(V.14)

Glory, grace, truth: Father, I desire that those also, whom you have given me, may be with me where I am, to see my glory, which you have given me because you loved me before the foundation of the world (John 17:24).From his fullness we have all received, grace upon grace. The law indeed was given through Moses; grace and truth came through Jesus Christ (John 1:16–17). But the hour is coming, and is now here, when the true worshippers will worship the Father in spirit and truth, for the Father seeks such as these to worship him. God is spirit, and those who worship him must worship in spirit and truth' (John 4:23–24). When the Spirit of truth comes, he will guide you into all the truth; for he will not speak on his own, but will speak whatever he hears, and he will declare to you the things that are to come (John 16:13). Pilate asked him, 'So you are a king?' Jesus answered, 'You say that I am a king. For this I was born, and for this I came into the world, to testify to the truth.

Everyone who belongs to the truth listens to my voice.' Pilate asked him, 'What is truth?' (John 18:37–38).

Dwell: Note the Jewish festival of Booths (= *skēnopēgia*, matching *eskēnosen* 'dwelt' in 1:14) was near (John 7:2).

(V. 15)
He existed before me: This is he of whom I said, 'After me comes a man who ranks ahead of me because he was before me' (John 1:30). Now a discussion about purification arose between John's disciples and a Jew. They came to John and said to him, 'Rabbi, the one who was with you across the Jordan, to whom you testified, here he is baptising, and all are going to him.' John answered, 'No one can receive anything except what has been given from heaven. You yourselves are my witnesses that I said, «I am not the Messiah, but I have been sent ahead of him.» He who has the bride is the bridegroom. The friend of the bridegroom, who stands and hears him, rejoices greatly at the bridegroom's voice. For this reason my joy has been fulfilled. He must increase, but I must decrease' (John 3:25–30). Jesus said to them, 'Very truly, I tell you, before Abraham was, I am' (John 8:58).

(V. 16)
Fullness: I came that they may have life, and have it abundantly (John 10:10). I have said these things to you so that my joy may be in you, and that your joy may be complete (John 15:11). But now I am coming to you, and I speak these things in the world so that they may have my joy made complete in themselves (John 17:13).

(V. 17)
Moses: Do not think that I will accuse you before the Father; your accuser is Moses, on whom you have set your hope. If you believed Moses, you would believe me, for he wrote about me (John 5:45–46). Then Jesus said to them, 'Very truly, I tell you, it was not Moses who gave you the bread from heaven, but it is my Father who gives you the true bread from heaven (John 6:32). Moses gave you circumcision (it is, of course, not from Moses, but from the patriarchs), and you circumcise

a man on the sabbath. If a man receives circumcision on the sabbath in order that the law of Moses may not be broken, are you angry with me because I healed a man's whole body on the sabbath?' (John 7:22–23). Then they reviled him, saying, 'You are his disciple, but we are disciples of Moses. We know that God has spoken to Moses, but as for this man, we do not know where he comes from' (John 9:28–29).

(V. 18)
Make known: Not that anyone has seen the Father except the one who is from God; he has seen the Father (John 6:46). I do not call you servants any longer, because the servant does not know what the master is doing; but I have called you friends, because I have made known to you everything that I have heard from my Father (John 15:15).'I have made your name known to those whom you gave me from the world. They were yours, and you gave them to me, and they have kept your word (John 17:6).'I made your name known to them, and I will make it known, so that the love with which you have loved me may be in them, and I in them' (John 17:26).

Pointers for prayer

a) John opens his gospel with a profound reflection on the meaning of creation, of life and of Jesus. Remember when you had a special awareness of the gift of life that filled you with gratitude to God for creation and the beauty and wonder of the world: 'All things came into being through him and without him not one thing came into being.'

b) We hear the Gospel message frequently. Sometimes it goes in one ear and out the other. Then there are occasions when it made us feel more alive, times when it helped us see the way ahead, like a light that shines in the darkness. Recall when the Gospel gave you hope in the midst of anxiety or sadness and helped you to see what action would be most life-giving for you and for others

c) Bring to mind people who have had a prophetic voice in the world – speaking the truth for the world to hear, a witness to testify to the light. Some of these may have been public figures. Others were ordinary people who have helped you see the 'light' by the witness of their own lives and words.

d) 'No one has ever seen God. It is the only Son of God, who is close to the Father's heart, who has made him known.' Jesus came to us to teach us about God and put a human face on God for us. For the people of his day, and for us, that was a mission of getting us to think again about how we see God and to believe in a God who is a God of love. Recall how the life and ministry of Jesus have changed your picture of God.

Prayer

God, most high, your only Son embraced the weakness of our flesh to give us the power to become your children; your eternal Word chose to dwell among us, that we might live in your presence.

Grant us a spirit of wisdom to know how rich is the glory you have made our own, and how great the hope to which we are called in Jesus Christ, the Word made flesh who lives and reigns with you in the unity of the Holy Spirit in the splendour of eternal light God for ever and ever. Amen.

Second Reading

Eph 1:3 Blessed be the God and Father of our Lord Jesus Christ, who has blessed us in Christ with every spiritual blessing in the heavenly places, [4] just as he chose us in Christ before the foundation of the world to be holy and blameless before him in love. [5] He destined us for adoption as his children through Jesus Christ, according to the good pleasure of his will, [6] to the praise of his glorious grace that he freely bestowed on us in the Beloved.

¹⁵ I have heard of your faith in the Lord Jesus and your love towards all the saints, and for this reason ¹⁶ I do not cease to give thanks for you as I remember you in my prayers. ¹⁷ I pray that the God of our Lord Jesus Christ, the Father of glory, may give you a spirit of wisdom and revelation as you come to know him, ¹⁸ so that, with the eyes of your heart enlightened, you may know what is the hope to which he has called you, what are the riches of his glorious inheritance among the saints, ¹⁹ *and what is the immeasurable greatness of his power for us who believe, according to the working of his great power.*

Initial observations

This reading offers us another opportunity within the Christmas season to reflect once more on what the birth of Jesus could mean for us today. While both parts of the reading do this, there is a special fervour in the second prayer. The air is invitatory: come and see what the Lord has done …

Kind of writing

In the genuine letters from Paul, the epistolary format has been adjusted to include a longer thanksgiving for the faith of the recipients. In 2 Corinthians, this takes the form of a 'blessing' prayer. In Ephesians, both styles are present.

vv. 3–14   Blessing prayer
vv. 15–23   Thanksgiving report

Our reading takes in excerpts from both. The entire passage should be read; it seems a pity that the lectionary needlessly omits v. 19. Sensibly, the Revised Common Lectionary offers vv. 3–14 as the reading.In contrast to the genuine letters, there is no implied account of what is happening in the community.

Origin of the reading

It is not quite sure if this letter should be addressed to the Ephesians, because some important manuscripts lack the expression 'in Ephesus'. It has also proved difficult to establish the context in community which occasioned the writing. (i) Is it to do with the famous and flourishing Artemis cult? (ii) Is it to do with proto-gnostic mythologies? (iii) Or, perhaps, some combination involving Jewish speculation on the heavenly journey? A clue is provided by the Dead Sea Scrolls, suggesting a Jew with a background in Jewish sectarianism. At the same time, the writing is very polished, so a Jew who enjoyed a good Hellenistic education (not unlike the apostle himself). Perhaps in a context of flourishing Judaism, the writer tries to bolster Christian identity. In any case, the vision is breathtaking, taking us well beyond the limits of the Roman Empire to a global expansion of the Gospel.

Related passages

> In our prayers for you we always thank God, the Father of our Lord Jesus Christ, for we have heard of your faith in Christ Jesus and of the love that you have for all the saints. (Colossians 1:3–4)

> I always thank my God as I remember you in my prayers, because I hear of your faith in the Lord Jesus and your love for all the saints. (Philemon 1:4–5)

Brief commentary

(V. 3)
Praise is the foundational attitude of prayer in the Bible, often taking the form 'blessed be God'. The expression 'every spiritual blessing' is especially rich: in contrast to human gifts, God's gift really is everything we need. It also places the Ephesians on the same level as the angels. The prayer will go on to describe Jesus in cosmic language; nevertheless, it begins with Jesus the Messiah.

(V. 4)

Christian vocation itself is to be found in the pre-existence of Christ, in whom we were already chosen in advance. The divine will is underlined in vv. 4–5, 9 and 11. The idea that all humanity is in view is also found in the Dead Sea Scrolls. 'In love' will be echoed in the 'beloved' of v. 6.

(Vv. 5–6)

Here the writer takes up the Pauline theme of adoption (Romans 8:15–23; Galatians 4:4–7). In contrast with Qumran, there is no reference at all to the predestination of the wicked. Predestination texts are also found in Paul: Romans 8:29–30 and 1 Corinthians 2:7. The pronouns are indicative: *he* and *his*. All is centred on God, a highly theocentric presentation of salvation. V. 6 tells us why all this took place: *to the praise of his glorious grace.*

(Vv. 15–16)

The reputation of the recipients is not boasting or flattery but a means of evangelisation, leading naturally to thanksgiving. Cf. 1 Thessalonians 1:3–12 and 2 Corinthians 8:1–2.

(V.17)

The writer moves from thanksgiving report to intercession. God's wisdom was already mentioned: *In him we have redemption through his blood, the forgiveness of our trespasses, according to the riches of his grace that he lavished on us. With* all wisdom and insight *he has made known to us the mystery of his will, according to his good pleasure that he set forth in Christ, as a plan for the fullness of time, to gather up all things in him, things in heaven and things on earth* (Ephesians 1:7–10). The Spirit of wisdom probably ought to have a capital letter, pointing to a more than human wisdom.

(V. 18)

The language here is very close to that of the Essenes: *May He enlighten your mind with wisdom for living, be gracious to you with the knowledge of eternal things, and lift up His gracious countenance upon you for everlasting peace* (1Qs [= The Community Rule] 2:3–4). The eyes of your heart is unparalleled elsewhere but seems to suggest moral conduct. The content of that enlightenment is expanded in terms of Christian hope. Saints means simply fellow Christians, as opposed to angels.

Pointers for prayer

a) How would my own prayer of blessing unfold? For what would I give thanks from the bottom of my heart?

b) The reputation of any community of faith is important – for the sake of the Gospel. Where does my community stand?

Prayer

God of wisdom and light, send your Holy Spirit into our hearts that we may be your children in name and in fact and thereby draw others into the great adventure of faith, hope and love in you. Through Christ our Lord. Amen.

🌿 First Reading 🌿

Sir 24:1   Wisdom praises herself,
      and tells of her glory in the midst of her people.

2   In the assembly of the Most High she opens her mouth,
      and in the presence of his hosts she tells of her glory:

8   'Then the Creator of all things gave me a command,
      and my Creator chose the place for my tent.
   He said, "Make your dwelling in Jacob,
      and in Israel receive your inheritance."

9   Before the ages, in the beginning, he created me,
      and for all the ages I shall not cease to be.

10   In the holy tent I ministered before him,
      and so I was established in Zion.

11   Thus in the beloved city he gave me a resting place,
      and in Jerusalem was my domain.

12   I took root in an honoured people,
      in the portion of the Lord, his heritage.'

Initial observations

Sirach 24 is one of the great texts for the personification of Lady Wisdom. Again, it would be a really good idea to read the whole text.

Kind of writing

The poem is laid out in three stanzas, with an introduction and a series of conclusions.

vv. 1–2	*Introduction*
vv. 3–7	(I) Pre-existent wisdom
vv. 8–12	(II) *Wisdom dwells in Jerusalem*
vv.13–17	(III) Horticultural metaphors
vv. 18–22	Viticulture and its fruits
vv. 23–29	Prose reflection
vv. 30–34	The poet's authority

Vv. 23–34 help us grasp the writer's goal, in two steps.

Prose reflection

> All this is the book of the covenant of the Most High God, the law that Moses commanded us as an inheritance for the congregations of Jacob. It overflows, like the Pishon, with wisdom, and like the Tigris at the time of the first fruits. It runs over, like the Euphrates, with understanding, and like the Jordan at harvest time. It pours forth instruction like the Nile, like the Gihon at the time of vintage. The first man did not know wisdom fully, nor will the last one fathom her. For her thoughts are more abundant than the sea, and her counsel deeper than the great abyss. (Sirach 24:23–29)

The poet's authority

> As for me, I was like a canal from a river, like a water channel into a garden. I said, 'I will water my garden and drench my flower-beds.' And lo, my canal became a river, and my river a

sea. I will again make instruction shine forth like the dawn, and I will make it clear from far away. I will again pour out teaching like prophecy, and leave it to all future generations. Observe that I have not laboured for myself alone, but for all who seek wisdom. (Sirach 24:30–34)

Origin of the reading

Sirach is a late Wisdom book, emphasising 'God in everything'. It was written in Hebrew – only partially extant – but it survives in its integrity in Greek.

Related passages

The passage seems to draw upon Proverbs 8, as well as Job 28. For another reflection on Wisdom, see Proverbs 1:20–33.

Wisdom cries out in the street; in the squares she raises her voice. At the busiest corner she cries out; at the entrance of the city gates she speaks: 'How long, O simple ones, will you love being simple? How long will scoffers delight in their scoffing and fools hate knowledge? Give heed to my reproof; I will pour out my thoughts to you; I will make my words known to you. Because I have called and you refused, have stretched out my hand and no one heeded, and because you have ignored all my counsel and would have none of my reproof, I also will laugh at your calamity; I will mock when panic strikes you, when panic strikes you like a storm, and your calamity comes like a whirlwind, when distress and anguish come upon you. Then they will call upon me, but I will not answer; they will seek me diligently, but will not find me. Because they hated knowledge and did not choose the fear of the LORD, would have none of my counsel, and despised all my reproof, therefore they shall eat the fruit of their way and be sated with their own devices. For waywardness kills the simple, and the complacency of fools destroys them; but those who listen to me will be secure and will live at ease, without dread of disaster.' (Proverbs 1:20–33)

Brief commentary

Every religion has to 'negotiate' the beyond and the nearness of God, his transcendence and his immanence, in technical vocabulary. Judaism achieved this by speaking of Wisdom, from the beyond in God, but present in all that exists.

(V. 1)
Praising yourself might seem strange but such poems are found widely ('aretologies'). 'Her people' points to Israel, where Wisdom 'made her dwelling'.

(V. 2)
Initially, we are in the heavenly court, where Wisdom exists already. The pre-existence of Wisdom is part of later Jewish theology and makes a really good link with the pre-existence of Christ in Ephesians.

(V. 8)
The reading was chosen in part because of the word tent (*skēnē*), also found in John 1:14 above. The language of dwelling etc. is picked up in the Prologue very well. A play of words is likely here because *skēnē* and *shekinah* sound similar. Cf. Proverbs 8:22. For a contrasting understanding: *Wisdom could not find a place in which she could dwell; but a place was found (for her) in the heavens. Then Wisdom went out to dwell with the children of the people, but she found no dwelling place. (So) Wisdom returned to her place and she settled permanently among the angels* (1 Enoch 42:1–2).

(V. 9)
In other writings, Wisdom seems to pre-exist before creation and even be the very mind of God. In any case, there is something of the divine about her.

(V. 10)

God's presence is recognised in the Temple in Jerusalem (a special interest of Sirach). The word 'tent' recurs. The verb 'to minister' is *leitourgeō*, related to our word liturgy.

(V. 11)

Concretely, Wisdom – the *shekinah* in the *skēnē* – is found in the Holy City, in the Holy of Holies, the heart of the Temple.

(V. 12)

Wisdom is present not only in the Temple but also in the Torah – a significant and breathtaking evolution. Cf. *All this is the book of the covenant of the Most High God, the law that Moses commanded us as an inheritance for the congregations of Jacob* (Sirach 24:23).

Pointers for prayer

a) God in all that is: recall your own awareness of how near the Lord is to us all – and give thanks.

b) Recall your own deep moments when the presence of God was somehow 'apparent' to you in his living word.

Prayer

God, closer to us than we are to ourselves and yet always greater than our hearts. Help us to remain in your presence: through your Wisdom in all creation and through Jesus, our wisdom and righteousness, our sanctification and redemption. Through the same Christ our Lord. Amen.

Themes across the readings

We continue to reflect on what happened for us in the birth of Jesus in Bethlehem. All the readings invite us to 'think big'. At the time that Ephesians was composed, the number of Christians around Ephesus was really small, but their hope, their vision was large. The closing prayer says it all: *May the God of our Lord Jesus Christ, the Father of glory, give you a spirit of wisdom and perception of what is revealed, to bring you to full knowledge of him. May he enlighten the eyes of your mind so that you can see what hope his call holds for you, what rich glories he has promised the saints will inherit.*

In contemporary theology, there is a great deal of exciting work on the cosmological implications of the vision of Ephesians and Colossians.

Chapter 11

Epiphany of the Lord C

Thought for the day

In our deepest selves, each of us is a mystery: Where do I come from? Where am I going? Why am I here? How should I live? The risk in our present culture is to sleepwalk through life, to be satisfied with a merely sentient, even material, existence. But the human 'project' is much greater. Each of us is really on a pilgrimage, or, better, on a quest – a quest to become my true self, in the image and likeness of God. My truest self is found by being open to God, in whom we live and move and have our being. By following that star, by listening to my conscience and inner self, I come home to God.

Prayer

You are the mystery at the heart of all that exists: draw us to yourself, O Lord, that knowing you we find our true selves, and finding our true selves, we may come to know you. Through Christ our Lord. Amen.

Gospel

Mt 2:1 In the time of King Herod, after Jesus was born in Bethlehem of Judea, wise men from the East came to Jerusalem, [2] asking, 'Where is the child who has been born king of the Jews? For we observed his star at its rising, and have come to pay him homage.' [3] When King Herod heard this, he was frightened, and all Jerusalem with him; [4] and calling together all the chief priests and scribes of the people, he inquired of them where the Messiah was to be born. [5] They told him, 'In Bethlehem of Judea; for so it has been written by the prophet:

[6] "And you, Bethlehem, in the land of Judah, are by no means least among the rulers of Judah; for from you shall come a ruler who is to shepherd my people Israel."'

[7] Then Herod secretly called for the wise men and learned from them the exact time when the star had appeared. [8] Then he sent them to Bethlehem, saying, 'Go and search diligently for the child; and when you have found him, bring me word so that I may also go and pay him homage.' [9] When they had heard the king, they set out; and there, ahead of them, went the star that they had seen at its rising, until it stopped over the place where the child was. [10] When they saw that the star had stopped, they were overwhelmed with joy. [11] On entering the house, they saw the child with Mary his mother; and they knelt down and paid him homage. Then, opening their treasure chests, they offered him gifts of gold, frankincense, and myrrh. [12] And having been warned in a dream not to return to Herod, they left for their own country by another road.

Initial observations

The readings from the Infancy Gospels bear an unusually close link to narratives in the Old Testament. Again, the writer is exploring the identity of Jesus, using citations and rewritten narratives. It all may seem strange to us, but the original hearers – Jewish Christians – would have had no trouble picking up the resonances and going straight to the meaning expressed in the stories. For us it takes a bit of work.

Kind of writing

As is usual with the infancy narratives, this is a kind of *haggadah*, a rabbinic style of writing which explores and exposes meaning by a resonant acoustic of echoes, thereby creating devotional and uplifting literature. Everything is in some way symbolic, the star, the Magi, the king, Bethlehem and the gifts, pointing to the identity of Jesus and the inclusion of the Gentiles in salvation.

Old Testament background

(i) Behind the story of the Magi – wise men – lies the story of Balaam from Numbers 22–24. In the Book of Numbers, an evil king of Moab tries to use the seer/magus Balaam to bring disaster on the people of Israel 'because they were so numerous'. Against God's will, Balaam obeys the king, but at the point of cursing Israel, Balaam utters an oracle of future hope. This oracle was read in later times as a Messianic promise:

'I see him, but not now; I behold him, but not near – a star shall come out of Jacob, and a sceptre shall rise out of Israel' (Numbers 24:17).

The author takes from this story the narrative of an evil king (Balak/Herod), trying to bring disaster (on Israel/on the Messiah), by means of Balaam (a seer/the Magi). The star in the story comes from Numbers 24:17 above and alerts the reader this time to Messianic fulfilment.

(ii) The gifts offered by the Magi call to mind a universalist text in Isaiah:

'A multitude of camels shall cover you, the young camels of Midian and Ephah; all those from Sheba shall come. They shall bring gold and frankincense, and shall proclaim the praise of the Lord' (Isaiah 60:6).

It was concluded from this text as well that the mode of transport of the Magi was camels, although Matthew supplies no such detail.

(iii) The Magi as a symbol of the Gentiles comes from an echo in Psalm 72:

'May the kings of Tarshish and of the isles render him tribute, may the kings of Sheba and Seba bring gifts. May all kings fall down before him, all nations give him service' (Psalm 72:10–11).

(iv) *Bethlehem, the city of David, is mentioned frequently in the Old Testament, unlike Nazareth. The proof text provided was, at the time, read as a messianic prophecy*:

'But you, O Bethlehem of Ephrathah, who are one of the little clans of Judah, from you shall come forth for me one who is to rule in Israel, whose origin is from of old, from ancient days' (Micah 5:2):

New Testament foreground

(i) Matthew's Gospel reflects the historical memory that Jesus did not himself directly evangelise the Gentiles, at least initially. 'These twelve Jesus sent out with the following instructions: "Go nowhere among the Gentiles, and enter no town of the Samaritans, but go rather to the lost sheep of the house of Israel" (Matthew 10:5–7).

(ii) Nevertheless, in Matthew's Gospel and community, the Gentiles are an important audience of the Good News: Matthew (x15); Mark (x6); Luke (x13); John (x5).

(a) *At the start of the ministry*: 'Now when Jesus heard that John had been arrested, he withdrew to Galilee. He left Nazareth and made his home in Capernaum by the sea, in the territory of Zebulun and Naphtali, so that what had been spoken through the prophet Isaiah might be fulfilled: "Land of Zebulun, land of Naphtali, on the road by the sea, across the Jordan, Galilee of the Gentiles – the people who sat in darkness have seen a great light, and for those who sat in the region and shadow of death light has dawned." From that time Jesus began to proclaim, "Repent, for the kingdom of heaven has come near."' (Matthew 4:12–17)

(b) *During the ministry*: 'When Jesus became aware of this, he departed. Many crowds followed him, and he cured all of them, and he ordered them not to make him known. This was to fulfil what had been spoken through the prophet Isaiah: 'Here is my servant, whom I have chosen, my beloved, with whom my soul is well pleased. I will put my Spirit upon him, and he will proclaim justice to the Gentiles. He will not wrangle or cry aloud, nor will anyone hear his voice in the streets. He will not break a bruised reed or quench a smouldering wick until he brings justice to victory. And in his name the Gentiles will hope.' (Matthew 12:15–21)

(c) *At the close of the Gospel*: 'Now, the eleven disciples went to Galilee, to the mountain to which Jesus had directed them. When they saw him, they worshipped him; but some doubted. And Jesus came and said to them, 'All, authority in heaven and on earth has been given to me. Go therefore and make disciples of all nations, baptising them in the name of the Father and of the Son and of the Holy Spirit, and teaching them to obey everything that I have commanded you. And remember, I am with you always, to the end of the age.' (Matthew 28:16–20)

St Paul

Now to God who is able to strengthen you according to my gospel and the proclamation of Jesus Christ, according to the revelation of the mystery that had been kept secret for long ages, but now is disclosed, and through the prophetic scriptures has been made known to all the nations, according to the command of the eternal God, to bring about the obedience of faith – to the only wise God, through Jesus Christ, be glory forever! Amen. (Romans 16:25–27; New English Translation slightly adjusted)

Brief commentary

Once the Old Testament correspondences and the Gospel anticipations have been uncovered the text practically comments itself. Nevertheless!

(V. 1)

This is King Herod the Great, who died in 4 BC. The 'wise men' are literally 'magi'. Magus, a Persian loan word, covers a range of meanings: wise man and priest, one who was expert in astrology, interpretation of dreams and various other occult arts. From the East: traditionally, the East was the source of wisdom.

(V.2)

The Gentiles identify universal hope in the Jewish Messiah and king.

(V. 3)

The historical Herod was quite paranoid about usurpers and even had some of his sons killed. Augustus said of him: 'I would prefer to be his pig (*hus*) than his son (*huios*).' This was after Herod put his two favourite sons, Aristobolus and Alexander, to death (he had already executed their mother, his favourite wife Mariamne). He was an exceptionally unstable, not to say murderous, spouse and parent.

(V. 5)

Matthew has Bible experts (like himself) identify the birthplace of the Messiah, with a proof-text from Micah. 'Shepherd' reminds us of David, the great symbol of God's faithfulness through time.

(V. 7)

The (f)rank hypocrisy of Herod links this symbolic tale with the massacre of the innocents to follow.

(V. 10)

Joy comes back in Matthew 28:8 at the empty tomb. For other uses, see Matthew 2:10; 13:20, 44; 25:21, 23.

(V.11)

The writer recalls Psalm 72 and Isaiah 60, as noted above.

(V.12)

With no further narrative use for them, the Magi are taken 'off stage' somewhat peremptorily.

Pointers for prayer

a) What is the star (the vision, hope or purpose) that lights up your journey?

b) Like the wise men, we do not travel our life journey alone. Who are the people who share your life journey now?

c) The wise men travelled bearing gifts. What gift do you bring with you on the journey?

d) At times the wise men lost sight of the star. What clouds have obscured your star?

e) Who, or what, might be Herod for you now? What forces, within or without, could subvert the dream or goal?

Prayer

Lord God of the nations, we have seen the star of your glory rising in splendour. The radiance of your incarnate Word pierces the darkness that covers the earth and signals the dawn of peace and justice. Make radiant the lives of your people with that same brightness, and beckon all the nations to walk as one in your light. We ask this through Jesus Christ, your Word made flesh, who lives and reigns with you in the unity of the Holy Spirit, in the splendour of eternal light, God for ever and ever. Amen.

🌿 Second Reading 🌿

Eph 3:1 *This is the reason that I Paul am a prisoner for Christ Jesus for the sake of you Gentiles–* [2] for surely you have already heard of the commission of God's grace that was given me for you, [3] and how the mystery was made known to me by revelation, as I wrote above in a few words, [4] *a reading of which will enable you to perceive my understanding of the mystery of Christ.* [5] In former generations this mystery was not made known to humankind, as it has now been revealed to his holy apostles and prophets by the Spirit: [6] that is, the Gentiles have become fellow heirs, members of the same body, and sharers in the promise in Christ Jesus through the gospel.

Initial observations

In the liturgical tradition, the epiphany embraces no fewer than three gospel stories: the Magi, the Baptism and the Wedding Feast at Cana. Each of these is a kind of disclosure or revelation. The feast, then, celebrates something 'being made known' or revealed and the reading from Ephesians is thus especially fitting.

Kind of writing

It can be tricky to follow the sequence of prayer and digression in Ephesians. In the view of many, Ephesians 3:2–13 forms a digression on the origin of Paul's gospel and apostleship. That is apparent from the abruptness of v. 2. V. 1 is itself an attempt to pick up a much earlier intercession from 1:16–19. But then 3:1 is subject to a digression, and the prayer will be completed only in 3:14–19. It may help to see a recomposed sequence as follows:

Eph 1:16 I do not cease to give thanks for you as I remember you in my prayers. [17] I pray that the God of our Lord Jesus Christ, the Father of glory, may give you a spirit of wisdom and revelation as you come to know him, [18] so that, with the eyes of your heart enlightened, you may know what is the hope to which he has called you, what are the riches of his glorious inheritance among the saints, [19] and what is the immeasurable greatness of his power for us who believe, according to the working of his great power.

Eph 3:1 This is the reason that I Paul am a prisoner for Christ Jesus for the sake of you Gentiles –

Eph 3:14 For this reason I bow my knees before the Father, [15] from whom every family in heaven and on earth takes its name. [16] I pray that, according to the riches of his glory, he may grant that you may be strengthened in your inner being with power through his Spirit, [17] and that Christ may dwell in your hearts through faith, as you are being rooted and grounded in love. [18] I pray that you may have the power to comprehend, with all the saints, what is the breadth and length and height and depth, [19] and to know the love of Christ that surpasses knowledge, so that you may be filled with all the fullness of God.

Origin of the reading

As noted elsewhere, there is a discussion about the Pauline authorship of this letter. A common solution is that the text was written by a disciple of Paul, after the apostle's death, to bring his teaching to bear in a new and later context. The reasons for doubting Pauline authorship include the vocabulary, the theology and the unusual relationship with the letter to the Colossians.

Related passages

But now in Christ Jesus you who once were far off have been brought near by the blood of Christ. For he is our peace; in his flesh he has made both groups into one and has broken down the dividing wall, that is, the hostility between us. He has abolished the law with its commandments and ordinances, that he might create in himself one new humanity in place of the two, thus making peace, and might reconcile both groups to God in one body through the cross, thus putting to death that hostility through it. So he came and proclaimed peace to you who were far off and peace to those who were near; for through him both of us have access in one Spirit to the Father. (Ephesians 2:13–18)

Brief commentary

(V.1)
The writer begins a prayer but it continues with the same words from v.14 onwards, 'for this reason'.

(V. 2)
The word commission can also be found here: as a *plan* for the fullness of time, to gather up all things in him, things in heaven and things on earth (Ephesians 1:10), and to make everyone see what is the plan of the mystery hidden for ages in God who created all things (Ephesians 3:9) .Thus, Paul's ministry is part of a wider commission or plan. This commission was given *to* Paul *for* others. It is presumed the hearers are familiar with Paul.

(V. 3)
Mystery is used in a different sense across the Pauline corpus and is evidently more common in the Deutero-Pauline letters: Romans 11:25; 16:25; 1 Corinthians 2:1, 7; 4:1; 13:2; 14:2; 15:51; *Ephesians 1:9; 3:3–4, 9; 5:32; 6:19; Colossians 1:26–27; 2:2; 4:3; 2 Thessalonians 2:7; 1 Timothy 3:9, 16.* It refers to the unity of Jews and Gentiles in the one people of God, already firmly established by the time of writing. See the important Ephesians 2:13–18 above. For revelation see Galatians 1:11–12, 15–16. Daniel 2 is also part of the background.

(V. 4)
Omitted in the lectionary for the sake of clarity, this verse sends the hearers back to the whole Pauline mission and theology. This grasp of

God's plan, entrusted to an individual, is then discerned and appropriated by the Church as whole.

(V. 5)

This amounts to a denial of a pattern found widely in the New Testament and in Paul, that is, that the Scriptures *foretell* and Christians then *confirm*. For our author, therevelation is new and made through the spiritual agents of the Christian community. Cf. I became its servant according to God's commission that was given to me for you, to make the word of God fully known, the mystery that has been hidden throughout the ages and generations but has now been revealed to his saints (Colossians 1:25–26).

(V. 6)

This verse compresses what has been said more fully in Ephesians 2:13–18. Note the vocabulary of heirs, body, promise and gospel, all genuine Pauline expressions. Cf. Ephesians 2:19. 'In' means 'by means of', an instrumental use.

Pointers for prayer

a) Disclosure and wonder are both present, inviting reflection on my own moments of revelation and awe.

b) On my own journey of faith, who have been the 'apostles', the ones sent who have helped me see the hope to which we are called?

Prayer

To pray, we use the closing verses of Romans 11 (vv. 33–36):

O the depth of the riches and wisdom and knowledge of God! How unsearchable are his judgments and how inscrutable his ways! For who has known the mind of the Lord? Or who has been his counsellor?' Or who has given a gift to him, to receive a gift in return?' For from him and through him and to him are all things. To him be the glory forever. Amen.

🌿 First Reading 🌿

Is 60:1 Arise, shine; for your light has come,
     and the glory of the LORD has risen upon you.
² For darkness shall cover the earth,
     and thick darkness the peoples;
   but the LORD will arise upon you,
     and his glory will appear over you.
³ Nations shall come to your light,
     and kings to the brightness of your dawn.
⁴ Lift up your eyes and look around;
       they all gather together, they come to you;
   your sons shall come from far away,
       and your daughters shall be carried in their nurses' arms.
⁵ Then you shall see and be radiant;
       your heart shall thrill and rejoice,
   because the abundance of the sea shall be brought to you,
       the wealth of the nations shall come to you.
⁶ A multitude of camels shall cover you,
       the young camels of Midian and Ephah;
       all those from Sheba shall come.
   They shall bring gold and frankincense,
       and shall proclaim the praise of the LORD.

Initial observations

As even a cursory glance will reveal, the reading is extremely well chosen. Firstly, because of the symbolism of light (more below). Secondly, because of the gathering/coming together of all the faithful. Following a very early intuition based on this text and Psalm 72, the reading adds pictorially both the *royal* status of the Magi and their mode of transport. The mention of gold and frankincense probably inspired the imaginative filling in of these details. Notice also that *three* places are mentioned (Matthew never says there were three Magi).

Kind of writing

The writing is poetry and in this case it is almost a textbook example of 'parallelism', whereby the second line repeats the first, but in more concrete, sometimes more elaborate vocabulary, for example vv. 1 and 2 or v.5.

Our excerpt comes from a longer section (Isaiah 60:1–62:12), and even within that the subsection 60:1–22 offers a poem on the light of the Lord. This is in response to Isaiah 59:9–10, which reads: Therefore justice is far from us, and righteousness does not reach us; we wait for light, and lo! there is darkness; and for brightness, but we walk in gloom. We grope like the blind along a wall, groping like those who have no eyes; we stumble at noon as in the twilight, among the vigorous as though we were dead.

Origin of the reading

Isaiah 60 comes from Third Isaiah, a prophet or prophets writing in the tradition of Isaiah of Jerusalem, but reflecting a much later situation after the return from the Exile in Babylon.

Related passages

> Then your light shall break forth like the dawn, and your healing shall spring up quickly; your vindicator shall go before you, the glory of the LORD shall be your rear guard. (Isaiah 58:8)

> … if you offer your food to the hungry and satisfy the needs of the afflicted, then your light shall rise in the darkness and your gloom be like the noonday. (Isaiah 58:10)

> Therefore justice is far from us, and righteousness does not reach us; we wait for light, and lo! there is darkness; and for brightness, but we walk in gloom. (Isaiah 59:9)

The sun shall no longer be your light by day, nor for brightness shall the moon give light to you by night; but the LORD will be your everlasting light, and your God will be your glory. Your sun shall no more go down, or your moon withdraw itself; for the LORD will be your everlasting light, and your days of mourning shall be ended. (Isaiah 60:19–20)

Brief commentary

To illustrate the theological integrity of this composite book, it may be sufficient to observe that there are many echoes, in the whole of Isaiah 60:1–22, of earlier passages in Isaiah.

(V. 1)
This text presumes that the Temple has been rebuilt and that all peoples will come there to worship. Here it is no longer God who will be their light: they themselves are light and they should shine. Cf. Matthew 5:14–15.

(V. 2)
After 2a, the repetition in 2b refers to the shadow of death or deadly darkness. The Lord's glory is not so much his splendour as the full presence of God.

(V. 3)
Notice the delightful evolution of the poetry: not just nations but also kings; not just light but also the brightness of your dawn.

(V. 4)
Cf. Isaiah 40:10–11. At this point, the addressees seem to be at home in Jerusalem, perhaps in the Temple. Very young children are envisaged.

(V. 5)
V. 5ab expresses the spontaneous joy, even exhilaration, at the prospect of salvation. V. 5cd might seem rather greedy, but it is an echo from the book of Exodus, reflecting the despoilment of the Egyptians before departure (Exodus 12:13–36). In any case, the bringing of gifts fits

the feast. Midian is associated with the Gulf of Aqaba, as is Ephah. Sheba is in Yemen, in the south-west of (modern) Arabia. In any case, a substantial distance is imagined.

(V. 6)

Cf. Isaiah 40:5. This is where we get the idea that camels are part of the story! The gold and frankincense of v.6c are intended for worship, as v.6d makes clear. Frankincense is a resin, mentioned in both the Old Testament and New Testament as a highly desired and esteemed product. The trade collapsed in the fifth century AD, after the Muslims forbade its use at funerals.

Pointers for prayer

a) Although the passage is indeed about light, it does acknowledge the need of light as we experience darkness. Not only do we need light, we are to *be* light, as Matthew 5 puts it.

b) The reading is exuberant, to a degree we might find hard to rise to, yet joy is truly part of our faith experience.

c) It all culminates in praise of the Lord, that spontaneous gratitude towards God who has loved us so much as to be one of us, the great mystery of Christmas.

d) The sense of pilgrimage, homecoming, is very much part of the reading and, of course, part of Christian imagination. Think only of *Pilgrim's Progress*. Reflect on your one journey of faith until today.

Prayer

We praise you, God, for the gift of light in creation, sunlight and moonlight, illuminating all you have made. Above all we thank you for the light of Christ, that you have shone in our hearts. May we welcome this light and became bearers of your light to all around us. Through Christ our Lord. Amen.

Themes across the readings

In the tradition, the Magi were later given names, personalities and biographies. The temptation to continue to 'fill in' proved irresistible. We may smile but the instinct is good because the Magi stand for real people – you and me – people on a spiritual quest, hearers of the word, listening out for a potential word from the Mystery, now disclosed.

Chapter 12

Baptism of the Lord C

Thought for the day

The great scenes in the Bible, precisely because of their greatness and, indeed, uniqueness, can be difficult to access personally. For the Baptism of Jesus, there are at least two potential approaches. Firstly, we could go back in our minds to a life-changing turning point in our own lives, so that we can speak of *before* and *after*. Secondly, we could also turn to our own experience when we felt deeply the affirmation of our identity and worth as 'the beloved' of someone. In the case of Jesus, these are combined: his identity and life are one, something we would like to be able say about ourselves too.

Prayer

Abba, Father, let us hear again today your words of affirmation to Jesus and in Jesus to us all. As your beloved sons and daughters, draw us more closely into your own life of love. Through Christ our Lord. Amen.

Gospel

Lk 3:15 As the people were filled with expectation, and all were questioning in their hearts concerning John, whether he might be the Messiah, [16] John answered all of them by saying, 'I baptise you with water; but one who is more powerful than I is coming; I am not worthy to untie the thong of his sandals. He will baptise you with the Holy Spirit and fire. [17] His winnowing fork is in his hand, to clear his threshing floor and to gather the wheat into his granary; but the chaff he will burn with unquenchable fire.'

[18] *So, with many other exhortations, he proclaimed the good news to the people.* [19] *But Herod the ruler, who had been rebuked by him because of Herodias, his brother's wife, and because of all the evil things that Herod had done,* [20] *added to them all by shutting up John in prison.*

[21] Now when all the people were baptised, and when Jesus also had been baptised and was praying, the heaven was opened, [22] and the Holy Spirit descended upon him in bodily form like a dove. And a voice came from heaven, 'You are my Son, the Beloved; with you I am well pleased.'

Initial observations

The baptism of Jesus by John is found in Mark, Matthew, Luke, the Acts and John. There are, however, differences in the reception and in the interpretation of the tradition. First of all the reception: Mark mentions the baptism without apparent difficulty, although he takes the trouble to locate John as Elijah, the one coming *before* the coming one; Matthew is very uncomfortable and inserts a dialogue in which John the Baptist objects to his baptising Jesus; Luke copes (!) by telling us before the baptism that John was in prison (see the verses above in italics, omitted in the lectionary reading); John gives only the phenomena around the baptism and actually leaves it out when you read the text carefully. All of this means that the baptism of Jesus by John is indisputably historical because Christians would not have made up a story that caused them so much unease and even embarrassment. It also means that the baptism was highly significant, both historically and theologically. Historically, the baptism marked the moment when Jesus accepted the role and preaching of the Baptist and at the same time began his own awareness of being the Son in a quite special way.

Theologically, each gospel interpreted the event in the light of the faith concerns at the time of writing. The details for Luke are in the comment below.

The link with the Baptist has more importance than is commonly recognised. It looks as if John the Baptist was a prophet who had departed to the desert and the Jordan, a move which implied some rejection of the Temple cult. He preached conversion of heart (*metanoia*), illustrated in a once-off immersion rite. His demanding ethics were offered in the light of the coming dreadful intervention/judgement of God. This can be seen in the passage above, which uses the traditional biblical image of harvest to convey the sorting and sifting of the end. What precisely John looked forward to is somewhat unclear: an angel, another prophet, God himself, the Messiah? It is historically likely that John proclaimed that the coming one would baptise with wind (*pneuma*) and fire (both images of judgement; cf. Psalm 1). The text was 'Christianised' by qualifying wind/spirit with 'holy', yielding Holy Spirit.

It need hardly be said that Christian baptism, that is the participation in the Easter Mystery and the gift of the Holy Spirit, is significantly different from John's baptism, a difference noticed in the New Testament itself:

> He had been instructed in the Way of the Lord; and he spoke with burning enthusiasm and taught accurately the things concerning Jesus, though he knew only the baptism of John. (Acts 18:25)

> Then he said, 'Into what then were you baptised?' They answered, 'Into John's baptism.' Paul said, 'John baptised with the baptism of repentance, telling the people to believe in the one who was to come after him, that is, in Jesus.' (Acts 19:3–4)

Kind of writing

We have here two short anecdotes (*chreiai*), linking the preaching of John and the baptism of Jesus.

Old Testament background

The wind

> The wicked are not so, but are like chaff that the wind drives away. (Psalm 1:4)

On the wicked he will rain coals of fire and sulphur; A scorching wind shall be the portion of their cup. (Psalm 11:6)

The dove

> Then he sent out the dove from him, to see if the waters had subsided from the face of the ground; but the dove found no place to set its foot, and it returned to him to the ark, for the waters were still on the face of the whole earth. So he put out his hand and took it and brought it into the ark with him. He waited another seven days, and again he sent out the dove from the ark; and the dove came back to him in the evening, and there in its beak was a freshly plucked olive leaf; so Noah knew that the waters had subsided from the earth. Then he waited another seven days, and sent out the dove; and it did not return to him any more. (Genesis 8:8–12)

New Testament foreground

Holy Spirit in Luke

Luke 1:15, 35, 41, 67; 2:25–27; 3:16, 22; 4:1, 14, 18; 10:21; 11:13; 12:10, 12.

> Then Jesus, filled with the power of the Spirit, returned to Galilee, and a report about him spread through all the surrounding country. (Luke 4:14)

> At that same hour Jesus rejoiced in the Holy Spirit and said, 'I thank you, Father, Lord of heaven and earth, because you have hidden these things from the wise and the intelligent and have revealed them to infants; yes, Father, for such was your gracious will. (Luke 10:21)

Prayer in Luke

In the Third Gospel, significant events are associated explicitly with prayer and in Luke Jesus prays about twice as often as in the other gospels. As well as in the Baptism scene here, we may note other places where Luke adds that it took place in a context of prayer:

Once when Jesus was praying alone, with only the disciples near him, he asked them, 'Who do the crowds say that I am?' (Luke 9:18)

Now about eight days after these sayings Jesus took with him Peter and John and James, and went up on the mountain to pray. And while he was praying, the appearance of his face changed, and his clothes became dazzling white. (Luke 9:28–29)

He was praying in a certain place, and after he had finished, one of his disciples said to him, 'Lord, teach us to pray, as John taught his disciples.' (Luke 11:1)

In his anguish he prayed more earnestly, and his sweat became like great drops of blood falling down on the ground. When he got up from prayer, he came to the disciples and found them sleeping because of grief, and he said to them, 'Why are you sleeping? Get up and pray that you may not come into the time of trial.' (Luke 22:44–46)

St Paul

And because you are children, God has sent the Spirit of his Son into our hearts, crying, 'Abba! Father!' So you are no longer a slave but a child, and if a child then also an heir, through God. (Galatians 4:6–7)

Brief commentary

(V.15)

This makes explicit the implied anxiety about the superiority of John who has given baptism to Jesus. For the reader of the gospel, this question has been already answered in Luke 1–2 by contrasting the roles of John the Baptist and Jesus the Messiah. The distinct stories collide at the Visitation, where the action of the prophet, still in the womb, identifies Jesus as Lord.

(Vv. 16–17)

By describing the coming one, John makes explicit his subordination to the one who is to come. Three points of contrast are drawn: John is not worthy, Jesus will baptise with the Spirit and he will bring judgement. Notice the three elements: water, wind (Spirit) and fire. The imagery of wind/spirit (*pneuma*) will be taken up in Acts 2, the story of Pentecost. Cf. the image of wind from Psalm 1 above.

(V. 18)

John's severe preaching of judgement is good news because it leads to conversion of heart and life.

(Vv. 19–20)

This is a very summary version of a longer story told in Mark and Matthew. Luke omits the martyrdom (except for Luke 9:9) but does underline the imprisonment in Luke 7:18–35. By leaving John in prison *before the baptism*, Luke does not deny John baptised Jesus but rather he shifts the spotlight adroitly from John to Jesus himself.

(V. 21)

It is noticeable that the baptism as such is consigned to a relative clause while the main sentence here is 'the heaven opened'. The opening of the heavens points to a new, unprecedented revelation.

(V. 22)

Bodily descent is difficult because there is no other way a dove *can descend*! Luke underlines in this way the objective reality of this descent by externalising it. The gospel writer also makes clear the new time of salvation by making Mark's metaphor of the dove into a *literal* evocation of the end of Noah's flood, marking a new time of salvation.

The voice from heaven declares the identity of Jesus as Son in a unique manner. The words combine Psalm 2:7 (common in the New Testament) and Isaiah 42:1 (the first Suffering Servant Song). Cf. Luke 9:35 at the Transfiguration.

Pointers for prayer

a) The people were searching and John pointed them in the direction of Jesus. On your life's journey who have been the John the Baptist people for you, people who have pointed you in the right direction?

b) The Baptism of Jesus was a very special moment for him that affirmed him in his identity as Son of God and in his mission. Recall the experiences that affirmed you – either in your sense of who you are, or in relation to the direction you were taking in life.

c) The Baptism of Jesus marks a transition point in his life, and the start of his public ministry. Recall the transition points in your own life. Where did you see the grace of God at work in those times?

d) This experience of Jesus occurred when he was at prayer. What part has prayer played in opening you to being aware of God in your life? What part has prayer played in helping you through a transition point in your life?

Prayer

Open the heavens, almighty Father, and pour out your Spirit upon your people gathered in prayer.

Renew the power of our baptismal cleansing and fill us with zeal for good deeds. Let us hear your voice once again, that we may recognise in your beloved Son our hope of inheriting eternal life. Grant this through Jesus Christ, your word made flesh, who lives and reigns with you in the unity of the Holy Spirit, in the splendour of eternal light, God for ever and ever. Amen.

🌿 Second Reading 🌿

Tit 2:11 For the grace of God has appeared, bringing salvation to all, [12] training us to renounce impiety and worldly passions, and in the present age to live lives that are self–controlled, upright, and godly, [13] while we wait for the blessed hope and the manifestation of the glory of our great God and Saviour, Jesus Christ. [14] He it is who gave himself for us that he might redeem us from all iniquity and purify for himself a people of his own who are zealous for good deeds.

[4] But when the goodness and loving kindness of God our Saviour appeared, [5] he saved us, not because of any works of righteousness that we had done, but according to his mercy, through the water of rebirth and renewal by the Holy Spirit. [6] This Spirit he poured out on us richly through Jesus Christ our Saviour, [7] so that, having been justified by his grace, we might become heirs according to the hope of eternal life.

Initial observations

The reading is appropriate also for the Baptism, following the ancient idea of the three 'epiphanies,' one to the Magi, one at the Baptism and another at Cana. The additional paragraph from chapter 3 brings the message of salvation into close proximity with the feast of the Baptism and invites direct reflection on our own baptism.

Kind of writing

For the letter layout of Titus, the reader is invited to go back to chapter 6, under the second reading. The letter to Titus offers three summaries or syntheses of the bynow traditional Pauline faith: Titus 1:1–4, 2:11–15 and 3:4–7. In other words, the two excerpts here are very well chosen for the feast. (Titus 2:11–14 is the second reading for Midnight Mass on Christmas Day; likewise, Titus 3:4–7 is the second reading for the Dawn Mass of Christmas Day).

Origin of the reading

The evolution of Christian 'churches', in the first ninety to one hundred years, may be mapped approximately as follows. The first thirty-year period (roughly 30–60) may be called the time of charism – charismatic leaders, adult conversion and the spiritual gifts. After the deaths of James, the son of Zebedee in AD 44, James, the brother of the Lord in 62 and Peter and Paul sometime around 65–67 under Nero, a different phase began which we may call that of memory or memorialisation. In the years 60–90, and certainly after the destruction of Jerusalem in AD 70, believers felt the need to consolidate the social memory and the oral tradition by writing gospels and by developing feasts and rites. In turn, this stage evolved into a third period, roughly 90–120, a time of institutionalisation: the definitive parting of the ways with Judaism, the appearance of hierarchical ministries and the development of ethics, church discipline and apologetics. (The schematisation can only be approximate.) The Pastoral Letters bridge the second and third of these periods, standing somewhere between memory and institution. The historical Paul was remembered for a very different generation.

Related passage

> From Paul, a slave of God and apostle of Jesus Christ, to further the faith of God's chosen ones and the knowledge of the truth that is in keeping with godliness, in hope of eternal life, which God, who does not lie, promised before time began. But now in his own time he has made his message evident through the preaching I was entrusted with according to the command of God our Saviour. To Titus, my genuine son in a common faith. Grace and peace from God the Father and Christ Jesus our Saviour! (Titus 1:1–4)

Brief commentary

Ch. 2:

(V. 11)

The baptism is regarded in the tradition as one of three epiphanies, along with the Epiphany proper and the wedding feast of Cana, read next Sunday. In Greek, the verb 'appeared' (*epephanē*) is given emphasis by its being placed first.

(V. 12)

As elsewhere in Titus, the writer contrasts two ways of living. The 'it' at the start refers back to the grace in the previous verse. The Greek word for training (*paideuousa*) is related to the culturally resonant world of Greek *paideia*, pointing to the education, maturation and enrichment of the whole person. The closing adverbs, hard to translate in English, say it all: living in a self-controlled way, a righteous way, a godly way.

(V. 13)

The first appearance (*epephanē*) will be completed by a second appearance (*epiphaneian*). Believers live between the 'already' and the 'not yet'. In this period of gestation, Christians are sustained by a *happy* hope. The word for happy (*makarian*) is the same one used in the Beatitudes in the gospels. *Makarios* stands somewhere between happy and blessed – perhaps 'flourishing' captures it best of all.

(V. 14)

The allusions to the genuine Paul are clear: 'Grace and peace to you from God the Father and our Lord Jesus Christ, who *gave himself for our sins* to rescue us from this present evil age according to the will of our God and Father, to whom be glory forever and ever! Amen' (Galatians 1:3–5). 'So the life I now live in the body, I live because of the faithfulness of the Son of God, who loved me and *gave himself for me*' (Galatians 2:20).

Ch. 3:

(V. 4)

The verb to appear is repeated (*epephanē*), linking this summary with the previous one. The coming of Christ is the appearance – epiphany – of God. It fits with the feast of the Baptism as a further disclosure of God's presence.

(V. 5)

The summary of Pauline teaching on justification and grace is quite accurate here, contrasting our efforts with God's mercy. Several expressions, however, are not from Paul, who never uses 'washing' and 'rebirth' and uses 'renewal' only once, in Romans 12:2. The way the sentence is written, it is clear that 'the washing of the new birth' and 'the renewing of the Holy Spirit' constitute a single experience.

(V. 6)
Again, while the teaching reflects that of Paul, the vocabulary is not really his. In Romans, Paul uses an alternative form of the verb to pour. 'Full measure' or 'richly' is post-Pauline (Colossians 3:16; 1 Timothy 6:17; Titus 3:6; 2 Peter 1:11). The genuine Paul calls Jesus saviour only once, in Philippians 3:20. By contrast, 'eternal life' in the next verse is genuinely Pauline: Romans 2:7; 5:21; 6:22–23; Galatians 6:8. Vv. 5–7 illustrate well the retrieval and reception of Paul in a later generation.

(V. 7)
This verse expresses well both Pauline teaching and the energy of the apostle. 'Confident expectation' translates as 'hope', a single word in Greek.

Pointers for prayer

a) Being baptised celebrates our conversion, our being changed in Christ. In the coming year, how do I see myself growing in discipleship?

b) We all have parts of our lives in need of purification, that is, in need of the healing, freedom and guidance of the Gospel. It might help to name these concretely for ourselves.

c) Salvation is one of those big words, loaded with history and feeling. Keep the reflection personal by asking how am I being saved (healed and set free) by Jesus at the present moment in my life?

Prayer

We praise your grace and goodness, your kindness and mercy to all of us in Jesus through the Holy Spirit. Help us to live the gifts of rebirth and renewal every day of our lives. Through Christ our Lord. Amen.

🌿 First Reading 🌿

Is 40:1   Comfort, O comfort my people,
   says your God.
2   Speak tenderly to Jerusalem,
      and cry to her
   that she has served her term,
      that her penalty is paid,
   that she has received from the LORD's hand
      double for all her sins.
3   A voice cries out:
   "In the wilderness prepare the way of the LORD,
      make straight in the desert a highway for our God.
4   Every valley shall be lifted up,
      and every mountain and hill be made low;
   the uneven ground shall become level,
      and the rough places a plain.
5   Then the glory of the LORD shall be revealed,
      and all people shall see it together,
      for the mouth of the LORD has spoken.'
9   Get you up to a high mountain,
      O Zion, herald of good tidings;
   lift up your voice with strength,
      O Jerusalem, herald of good tidings,
      lift it up, do not fear;
   say to the cities of Judah,
      'Here is your God!'
10   See, the Lord GOD comes with might,
      and his arm rules for him;
   his reward is with him,
      and his recompense before him.
11   He will feed his flock like a shepherd;
      he will gather the lambs in his arms,
   and carry them in his bosom,
      and gently lead the mother sheep.

Initial observations

At the close of the Christmas season, it might seem strange to find Isaiah 40 as our reading. However, in the year of Luke, Isaiah is not read in the Sunday readings of Advent in year C; in any case, it is a fitting reading to match the story of the Baptism.

Kind of writing

This is poetry, as usual. The reader will not fail to notice piling up of significant synonyms to get the message across: (i) term, penalty, double; (ii) comfort, speak tenderly; (iii) might, arm, reward, recompense; (iv) feed, gather, carry, gently lead; (v) interspersed are terms full of emotion: get up, lift, say, see. The core message remains 'Here is your God!'

Origin of the reading

The reading is from Second Isaiah, an anonymous prophet or a series of prophets, whose work is represented in Isaiah 40–55 (some think up to ch. 66). These oracles were spoken, for the most part, just before the end of the great Exile in Babylon.

The term 'good news' calls for special comment. This term (interestingly always a verb in the Old Testament) usually meant ordinary secular good news. But in Isaiah, it points to the good news of God's end-time gift of salvation to his people. John the Baptist and Jesus most likely take the term from Isaiah.

Related passage

> How beautiful upon the mountains are the feet of the messenger who announces (lit. who brings good news) peace, who brings good news, who announces salvation, who says to Zion, 'Your God reigns.' (Isaiah 52:7; also Isaiah 60:6 and 61:1)

Brief commentary

(V. 1)

The opening words convey the compassionate tone of Second Isaiah. The double command to comfort is surely significant.

(V. 2)

The parallel words (term, penalty, double) reflect the reading of the Exile in Babylon as both punishment and purification. Writing towards the very end of the Exile in 539 BC, the writer offers a vision of hope.

(V. 3)

The voice is to cry out – but not in the wilderness, as in the Gospel reception of this text. Instead, the prophet proclaims *in Babylon* what they must do to prepare a way for the Lord. Notice the implied acknowledgement that God was with them all along in the Exile, even though they may not have always been aware of that.

(V. 4)

Imagery from what we would call engineering serves to illustrate the saving journey home. We are to imagine a return using the fertile crescent, along the banks of the Euphrates.

(V. 5)

Glory in the Hebrew Bible points to God's presence and action, rather than simply honour and exaltation. That all people (all flesh, literally) will see God's accompaniment of his people shows the universal vision of Second Isaiah.

(V. 9)

In context, these verses sound like the call reported in Second Isaiah. In the Greek translation, 'herald of good tidings' is rendered by a single word, *euaggelizomenos*, related our word gospel (*euaggelion*). 'Do not fear' is the ever-present reassurance given to the faithful (at least 128 times in the entire Bible).

(V. 10)

Notice the parallelism of might/arm and reward/recompense. These last two correspond to the earlier term penalty/double.

(V. 11)

Here is a remarkable and appealing pastoral image, often set to music. The imagery already had a long history before Second Isaiah was written and, of course, it comes up powerfully in the New Testament (Luke 15, John 10, for example). The shepherd is almost motherly to the mother ewes. Again in the Greek translation, the very last word is 'comfort' (*parakalesei*), echoing verse 1.

Pointers for prayer

a) Very difficult experiences can leave us wondering about God. Where is God? Why this? And yet, with steadfastness, we come to see the hand of God. When has this been true for you?

b) The reading resonates with the term good news. In our culture, we hesitate – and still, the Christian Gospel is at its heart astonishingly good Good News. When have I felt this myself?

c) The image of caring invites personal reflection. Who has care for/cares for me? For whom do I care? This is really an experience of being loved. When have I felt God carrying me?

Prayer

God, all compassionate and all loving, we believe that everything from your hand is for our good, even when we cannot see it at the time. Help us to place our trust in you, our good shepherd, as you carry us through life. Through Christ our Lord. Amen.

Themes across the readings

From quite early Christian tradition, John was identified with the voice crying in the wilderness. Vv. 9–11 are appropriate: the herald is called upon to point out the coming one. Psalm 104 (103) is a joyful response to the first reading. It is especially suitable because it mentions messengers (first reading) and the Holy Spirit (Gospel).

Chapter 13

Second Sunday of Year C

Thought for the day

The (extra)ordinary experience of 'everyday' love is itself a sacrament. As such, it mediates the love of God and gives us both an experience and a language by which we may speak of God, God who is love itself.

Prayer

Open our eyes to recognise you at the heart of the 'everyday' love that sustains and inspires us: whoever lives in love, lives in God and God in them! Through Christ our Lord. Amen.

🍃 Gospel 🍃

Jn 2:1 On the third day there was a wedding in Cana of Galilee, and the mother of Jesus was there. [2] Jesus and his disciples had also been invited to the wedding. [3] When the wine gave out, the mother of Jesus said to him, 'They have no wine.' [4] And Jesus said to her, 'Woman, what concern is that to you and to me? My hour has not yet come.' [5] His mother said to the servants, 'Do whatever he tells you.' [6] Now standing there were six stone water jars for the Jewish rites of purification, each holding twenty or thirty gallons. [7] Jesus said to them, 'Fill the jars with water.' And they filled them up to the brim. [8] He said to them, 'Now draw some out, and take it to the chief steward.' So they took it. [9] When the steward tasted the water that had become wine, and did not know where it came from (though the servants who had drawn the water knew), the steward called the bridegroom [10] and said to him, 'Everyone serves the good wine first, and then the inferior wine after the guests have become drunk. But you have kept the good wine until now.' [11] Jesus did this, the first of his signs, in Cana of Galilee, and revealed his glory; and his disciples believed in him.

Initial observations

This is the opening act of the ministry in the Fourth Gospel. As such, it corresponds in some manner to accounts we find in Mark 1:14 or Luke 4:16–30. It is a foundational tableau, which sets the scene for the unfolding of Jesus' identity and ministry in John's Gospel. In ancient tradition, the Epiphany, Baptism and Cana were all regarded as one combined revelatory event; hence John 2 is read today instead of Luke (the gospel for the year).

Kind of writing

This story is the Johannine reception and interpretation of chiefly nuptial imagery, taken from the Hebrew Bible and the ministry and teaching of Jesus. There are historical and even theological problems with taking the story literally.

(i) The Cana story has no corresponding miracle in the Synoptic tradition. (ii) It does not follow the usual pattern of problem, encounter, request, word, healing, proof. (iii) The vocabulary is entirely Johannine. (iv) The theological 'tone' is purely Johannine, with a link to the call stories, as well as a link with the Woman at the Well. (v) The role of the unnamed mother is entirely exceptional and invites reading at another level.

Old Testament background

The gospel passage uses three metaphors familiar from the Old Testament and the wider Jewish literature of the time: (i) feast, (ii) wedding and (iii) wine.

(i) On this mountain the LORD of hosts will make for all peoples a feast of rich food, a feast of well-aged wines, of rich food filled with marrow, of well-aged wines strained clear. And he will destroy on this mountain the shroud that is cast over all peoples, the sheet that is spread over all nations; he will swallow up death forever. Then the LORD God will wipe away the tears from all faces, and the disgrace of his people he will take away from all the earth, for the LORD has spoken. It will be said on that day, Lo, this is our God; we have waited for him, so that he might save us. This is the LORD for whom we have waited; let us be glad and rejoice in his salvation. For the hand of the LORD will rest on this mountain. (Isaiah 25:6–10) Cf. Amos 9:13–14; Jeremiah 31:12. Proverbs 9:1–6; Sirach 24:19–21.

Also, some intertestamental literature is a help, such as:
And in those days the whole earth will be worked in righteousness, all of her planted with trees, and will find a blessing. And they shall plant pleasant trees upon her – vines. And he who plants vines upon here will produce wine for plenitude. And every seed that is sown on her, one measure will yield a thousand (measures) and one measure of olives will yield ten measures of presses of oil. (1 Enoch 10:18–19)

For at that time I shall only protect those found in this land at that time. And it will happen that when all that which should come to pass in these parts has been accomplished, the Anointed One will begin to be revealed. And Behemoth will reveal itself from its place, and Leviathan will come from the sea, the two great monsters which I created on the fifth day of creation and which I shallhave kept until that time. And they will be nourishment for all who are left. The earth will also yield fruits ten thousandfold. And on one vine will be a thousand branches, and one branch will produce a thousand clusters, and one cluster will produce a thousand grapes, and one grape will produce a cor of wine. (2 Baruch 29:2–5; 1 cor was the equivalent of 230 litres!)

(ii) Do not fear, for you will not be ashamed; do not be discouraged, for you will not suffer disgrace; for you will forget the shame of your youth, and the disgrace of your widowhood you will remember no more. For your Maker is your husband, the LORD of hosts is his name; the Holy One of Israel is your Redeemer, the God of the whole earth he is called. For the LORD has called you like a wife forsaken and grieved in spirit, like the wife of a man's youth when she is cast off, says your God. For a brief moment I abandoned you, but with great compassion I will gather you. In overflowing wrath for a moment I hid my face from you, but with everlasting love I will have compassion on you, says the LORD, your Redeemer. (Isaiah 54:4–8; cf. Isaiah 62:4–5; Jeremiah 2:2; 3:1–12; Hosea 1–2; Ezekiel 16 and 23; Song of Songs *passim*)

(iii) I will restore the fortunes of my people Israel, and they shall rebuild the ruined cities and inhabit them; they shall plant vineyards and drink their wine, and they shall make gardens and eat their fruit (Amos 9:14; cf. Numbers 13:23; Isaiah 16:10; 24:7–12; 25:6–8; Jeremiah 48:33; Joel 1:5, 7, 11–13; Psalm 4:7; 104:15; Wine and love: Song 1:2, 4; 2:4, 10; 5:1; 7:10; 8:2).

New Testament foreground

We recall the many parables that use the language of wedding, feast and vineyard.

Now John's disciples and the Pharisees were fasting; and people came and said to him, 'Why do John's disciples and the disciples of the Pharisees fast, but your disciples do not fast?' Jesus said to them, 'The *wedding guests* cannot fast while the *bridegroom* is with them, can they? As long as they have the *bridegroom* with them, they cannot fast. The days will come when the *bridegroom* is taken away from them, and then they will fast on that day. No one sews a piece of unshrunk cloth on an old cloak; otherwise, the patch pulls away from it, the new from the old, and a worse tear is made. And no one puts new *wine* into old wineskins; otherwise, the *wine* will burst the skins, and the *wine* is lost, and so are the skins; but one puts new *wine* into fresh wineskins.' (Mark 2:18–22)

He who has the bride is the bridegroom. The friend of the bridegroom, who stands and hears him, rejoices greatly at the bridegroom's voice. For this reason my joy has been fulfilled. (John 3:29) Cf. John 4 (a nuptial scene) plus the burial of Jesus, with echoes of the Song of Songs (John 19:38–42).

Marriage symbolism is taken up in John 2–4 with an important if very gentle echo at the burial of Jesus. In John's Gospel, Jesus' body is prepared for burial as follows: Nicodemus, who had at first come to Jesus by night, also came, bringing a mixture of myrrh and aloes, weighing about a hundred pounds (John 19:39). The excessive quantity indicates a kingly burial. The ingredients – myrrh and aloes – are found together in the Old Testament only in nuptial contexts (Psalm 45:8; Proverb 7:17; Song 4:14).

St Paul

'For this reason a man will leave his father and mother and be joined to his wife, and the two will become one flesh.' This is a great mystery, and I am applying it to Christ and the church. (Ephesians 5:31–32)

Brief commentary

(V. 1)

The time doesn't quite link up with the other 'days' and represents in some fashion the time of salvation (Exodus 19:11; Genesis 22:4; Hosea 6:2). It may link to the 'very soon' of the previous scene. The mother is present in this gospel in symbolic role, that is, representing the mother religion (as also at the crucifixion in the Fourth Gospel only).

(V. 2)
The disciples are important 'witnesses' at the start and at the end. Their presence at the start and at the end also links this story to the previous call story in a significant way.

(V. 3)
Lack of wine points to lack of true joy. In the eyes of the writer and his community, the mother religion has run out of the source of true joy (joy is a large theme in John and 1 John).

(V. 4)
A hesitation (rejection?) is found also in the story of the royal official. Yet the initial refusal is overcome. The hour is a strong Johannine theme and links immediately with the events of salvation. Cf. Jesus said to her, 'Woman, believe me, the hour is coming when you will worship the Father neither on this mountain nor in Jerusalem (John 4:21).'Very truly, I tell you, the hour is coming, and is now here, when the dead will hear the voice of the Son of God, and those who hear will live'(John 5:25). Then they tried to arrest him, but no one laid hands on him, because his hour had not yet come (John 7:30). Now before the festival of the Passover, Jesus knew that his hour had come to depart from this world and go to the Father (John 13:1).

(V. 5)
Notice again that the principals (bride and groom) are not involved.

(V. 6)
These enormous ritual containers stand for the Jewish faith as received and practised. It matters that they are jars precisely for Jewish rites of purification – some kind of transformation in faith is taking place.

(V. 7)
To fill has a special use in this gospel as well: So they gathered them up, and from the fragments of the five barley loaves, left by those who had

eaten, they filled twelve baskets (John 6:13). This makes a link between the wine and the bread.

(V. 8)

To draw (as in water) is a rare word in the New Testament: A Samaritan woman came to draw water, and Jesus said to her, 'Give me a drink' (John 4:7). The woman said to him, 'Sir, give me this water, so that I may never be thirsty or have to keep coming here to draw water' (John 4:15). This makes an important link with this 'meeting your future wife at a well' scene in this gospel.

(V. 9)

Where it came from (*pothen*, in Greek): this is a key word and topic across the Fourth Gospel regarding the apparent and real origins of Jesus: 'Yet we know where this man is from; but when the Messiah comes, no one will know where he is from' (John 7:27–28). 'We know that God has spoken to Moses, but as for this man, we do not know where he comes from' (John 9:29–30). Pilate entered his headquarters again and asked Jesus, 'Where are you from?' (John 19:9). The servants (= disciples) know the true origin of Jesus. It seems clear at this point that Jesus himself is the real bridegroom.

(V. 10)

The now is the now of salvation: But the hour is coming, and is now here, when the true worshippers will worship the Father in spirit and truth, for the Father seeks such as these to worship him. (John 4:23)

(V.11)

First (*archē*, meaning source); sign (*sēmeion*, the word for miracle in the Fourth Gospel); glory (*doxa*, a large theme in the gospel. To believe is a vast theme too, occurring some ninety-nine times: ninety-eight times as a verb, never as a noun (interestingly) and only once as an adjective: *Then he said to Thomas, 'Put your finger here and see my hands. Reach out your hand and put it in my side. Do not doubt but believe'* (John 20:27, lit. 'be not unbelieving but believing'). In this way, the gospel indicates that we believe in a person, not in doctrines.

Pointers for prayer

a) The marriage imagery puts all the emphasis on love, an emphasis found richly in this gospel, in St Paul and, of course, in Jesus' own teaching. Go back to significant experiences of being loved and how these have opened your own heart to receive and to give in love.

b) The wine symbolises true joy in believing – a bit of a challenge these days, but central nevertheless and even life-giving. Where do you find your springs of joy?

c) 'Do whatever he tells you' is a strong invitation to conformity to Christ on the path of discipleship. What have been the important points on that path? And where am I now?

Prayer

God of wonders, at Cana in Galilee, you revealed your glory in Jesus Christ and summoned all humanity to life in him. Show to your people gathered on this day your transforming power and give us a foretaste of the wine you keep for the age to come. We make our prayer through our Lord Jesus Christ, your Son, who lives and reigns with you in the unity of the Holy Spirit, God for ever and ever. Amen.

Second reading

1 Cor 12:4 Now there are different gifts, but the same Spirit. [5] And there are different ministries, but the same Lord. [6] And there are different results, but the same God who produces all of them in everyone. [7] To each person the manifestation of the Spirit is given for the benefit of all. [8] For one person is given through the Spirit the message of wisdom, and another the message of knowledge according to the same Spirit, [9] to another faith by the same Spirit, and to another gifts of healing by the one Spirit, [10] to another performance of miracles, to another prophecy, and to another discernment of spirits, to another different kinds of tongues, and to another the interpretation of tongues. [11] It is one and the same Spirit, distributing as he decides to each person, who produces all these things.

Initial observations

It may seem odd that, at the effective start of Year C, we plunge straight into ch. 12 of 1 Corinthians without further notice. It is likely that the choice was inspired by the Week of Prayer for Christian Unity, providing us with very fitting reflections from St Paul this Sunday and next Sunday.

Kind of writing

From time to time, Paul lays out his argument in a concentric pattern. Over chapters 12–14 this happens *more than once*. It happens across the three chapters, 12 and 14 being the outside and 13 being the inside. But it also happens within each of the chapters. Becoming aware of this is not a matter of literary games, but rather attaining a grasp of the clear sequence of complex ideas. Thus:

Overall plan of 1 Corinthians 12–14

A	B	A*
Diversity	Love	Order
ch. 12	ch. 13	ch. 14

In this scheme, the key to the solution is really ch. 13, occupying a central place in two senses. The *issue* is raised in 12; the *criterion* is explored in 13; the criterion is *applied* in 14. So the argument is both concentric and linear.

Within chapter 12

a	b	a*
Charisms, prophecy, tongues	The body	Charisms, prophecy, tongues
12:4–11	12:12–26	12:27–31

In this scheme, the disorder of competitiveness is resolved using the metaphor of the body, showing that differences should ideally be complementary. Again, the argument is both concentric and linear: the *issue* raised in vv. 4–11 is *resolved* in vv. 27–31 in light of the *principle* in vv. 12–26.

Our reading from the lectionary sensibly matches the divisions outlined above.

Origin of the reading

The context is Corinth, where there seems to have been a highly developed sense of competition among the few Corinthians who were Christ-believers. This showed itself particularly in the spiritual gifts. Those with the more exuberant expressions of prayer were evidently regarded more highly. In Paul's mind, this is simply dangerous, attaching far too great an importance to the external manifestation of an internal reality. Furthermore, it is leading to divisions and to scandal. Why scandal? In 1 Corinthians 14, Paul imagines a case where a non-believer attends the worship of the community. If it is all tongues etc., this poor visitor will be left totally flummoxed and will leave without having heard helpful word for his or her life (see below under related passages).

Related passages

> Now concerning spiritual gifts, brothers and sisters, I do not want you to be uninformed. You know that when you were pagans, you were enticed and led astray to idols that could not speak. Therefore I want you to understand that no one speaking by the Spirit of God ever says 'Let Jesus be cursed!' and no one can say 'Jesus is Lord' except by the Holy Spirit. (1 Corinthians 12:1–3)

> If, therefore, the whole church comes together and all speak in tongues, and outsiders or unbelievers enter, will they not say that you are out of your mind? But if all prophesy, an

unbeliever or outsider who enters is reproved by all and called to account by all. After the secrets of the unbeliever's heart are disclosed, that person will bow down before God and worship him, declaring, 'God is really among you.' (1 Corinthians 14:23–25) (There is another gift list in Romans 12:6–8.)

Brief commentary

(Vv. 1–3)
'Jesus is Lord' is the foundational acclamation common to all, relativising all other status-raising 'spiritual' claims.

(Vv. 4–6)
'Varieties' would be better rendered 'apportionings' to suggest allotting by God. Paul prefers the word 'charisms' (the *charismata*) to 'spiritual gifts' (the *pneumatika*), because the latter is associated with status rivalry, whereas charism means gift, something received. Already, diversity is secondary to unity. Notice the incipiently trinitarian frame, pointing to the one God as giver.

(V. 7)
The argument begins with this practical application of a general principle.

(V. 8)
Wisdom can be pejorative in this letter; here it means wisdom *from God*. Knowledge is also tricky; here it means a word spoken under God's inspiration, and hence positive in the context.

(V. 9)
Faith here *cannot* mean the saving faith that all believers enjoy. It means some extraordinary 'feat' of faith *for the benefit of others*. As a good corrective, see 1 Corinthians 13:2!

(V. 10)
These different gifts return in ch. 14 when Paul considers the good order of worship and the *relative* importance of tongues.

(V.11)

This first argument is concluded and framed by a reference back to the one Spirit who gives to all. The vocabulary synthesises the principles and gifts mentioned in vv. 4–10. Finally, the Spirit's *choice* annuls any claim to status on the basis of one's 'spirituality'.'

Pointers for prayer

a) All gifts are precisely gifts and not grounds for status or self-congratulation. Status, as a temptation, is not unknown in the Church, alas.

b) All gifts are for the community as a whole and not first of all for the individual. Gifts are for mutual building up and not first of all for private delectation.

Prayer

Gracious giver of all the gifts, guide us to recognise you at the heart of all our energies and talents; help us to use all you have given for the benefit of others. Through Christ our Lord. Amen.

🌿 First reading 🌿

Is 62:1   For Zion's sake I will not keep silent,
      and for Jerusalem's sake I will not rest,
  until her vindication shines out like the dawn,
      and her salvation like a burning torch.
2   The nations shall see your vindication,
      and all the kings your glory;
  and you shall be called by a new name
      that the mouth of the Lord will give.
3   You shall be a crown of beauty in the hand of the Lord,
      and a royal diadem in the hand of your God.
4   You shall no more be termed Forsaken,
      and your land shall no more be termed Desolate;

but you shall be called My Delight Is in Her,
    and your land Married;
for the LORD delights in you,
    and your land shall be married.
5   For as a young man marries a young woman,
    so shall your builder marry you,
and as the bridegroom rejoices over the bride,
    so shall your God rejoice over you.

Initial observations

As the extended comment on John 2:1–11 makes clear, this passage
is a rich illustration of 'nuptial symbolism' from the Hebrew Bible. It
is also a thrilling example of both biblical poetry and the theology of
love.

Kind of writing

The excerpt shows the usual marks of biblical poetry: parallelism
and metaphors. The parallelism is especially clear. Apart from the
matrimonial/love metaphors, there is nature (dawn), royalty (crown,
diadem) and construction/engineering (builder).

The full context is all of Isaiah 61:1–62:12, closing with a resumption
of the earlier metaphors: They shall be called, 'The Holy People, The
Redeemed of the Lord'; and you shall be called, 'Sought Out, A City
Not Forsaken' (Isaiah 62:12).

Ch. 62 divides as follows:

62:1–5	Jerusalem as a bride
62:6–9	The sentinels of the city
62:10–12	The city welcomes the victor

Origin of the reading

The reading comes from Third Isaiah, written very probably after the
return from Exile. It was a challenging time because the rebuilding

did not happen as quickly as some had hoped. We might even call it a period of 'failed reconstruction', not unlike our own.

Related passages

The Old Testament and intertestamental background is as given above for John 2:1–11. In addition: jewellery.

> O afflicted one, storm-tossed, and not comforted, I am about to set your stones in antimony, and lay your foundations with sapphires. I will make your pinnacles of rubies, your gates of jewels, and all your wall of precious stones. (Isaiah 54:11–12)

We may also note, there are many points of contact with Isaiah 49, 51–52 and 54.

Brief commentary

The poem as a whole celebrates the vindication and restoration of Jerusalem.

(V. 1)

Why the concern with 'vindication' at this point? The Jerusalem Bible uses 'integrity' for the same Hebrew word usually translated as justification. The great promise of Isaiah 61 is grounded in the specific history of the Israelites. The promise of general justice is made real in God's restoration of Israel, now raised up as a light for the nations.

Zion, a part of the city, stands for Jerusalem as a Davidic city (destroyed in 587 bc). The speaker is unable to hold in the good news any longer. The dawn, a measure of her future beauty, symbolises the salvation to God, just as the torch suggests victory over darkness. The king as both bridegroom and as the sun is culturally very ancient.

(V. 2)

A new name in the Bible always suggests a new reality, a new relationship with God. Cf. Isaiah 60:14–17, 61:3, 6; 62:4, 12. The giving of the new name is so that she will be recognised and established. The restoration will be a public vindication and a fulfilment of the promises in Isaiah 61:5–7.

(V. 3)

The royal imagery evokes the Davidic monarchy. Cf. *Come out. Look, O daughters of Zion, at King Solomon, at the crown with which his mother crowned him on the day of his wedding, on the day of the gladness of his heart* (Song 3:11).

(V. 4)

The key here is the contrasting terms: forsaken and desolate, like an abandoned wife, in contrast with the newly married status of 'my delight is in her' and 'married'. This reflects the marriage of the deity and the city, common in the religious practice of the time. For abandoned, see Isaiah 49:14; 54:1, 4; 60:15. For desolate, see Isaiah 49:8.

(V. 5)

In this verse, God is explicitly identified as the bridegroom. The imagery is very free and full of joy. Some translations (Jewish Publication Society, New International Version) read 'your sons (*bānāyik*) shall marry you', which is contrary to the sense and culturally inappropriate. With the New Revised Standard Version and the lectionary, we read builder (*bōnēk*).

Pointers for prayer

a) The writer has wonderful news and can't keep it in. When did you last feel like that? This happens to us too, not only in 'ordinary' experience, but also in faith, and it leads to the desire to spread our good news.

b) In the past, perhaps you have experienced the life-giving transition from feeling forsaken to be being loved. A prayer of relief and thanksgiving.

c) Perhaps we do not think often enough of God rejoicing over us. It is a wonderful image and may help restore some of the joy in believing.

Prayer

God, our great lover, we believe that you brought us into being, that you love us and that you take delight in us.

Open in our hearts as great a love for you and as joyful a delight in our God, in whom we live and move and have our being. Through Christ our Lord. Amen.

Themes across the readings

The first reading is an ideal preparation for understanding the Cana story against its biblical background. In particular, the notes of joy and delight are taken up in the gospel scene. The psalm echoes the joy and the royal imagery of the first reading. The whole ensemble is a great challenge to us today, when believing is marked more by anguish and anxiety than by joy and exhilaration. It is, perhaps, not an accident that the writings in the New Testament that are strongest on joy are also strongest on prayer and the Holy Spirit: Paul, Luke–Acts and John. Here is something for us today ...

The Table of the Faith

As we look ahead to the future of faith, especially here in Ireland, Jesus' own practice of table-fellowship can inspire us. In this short reflection, the 'table of the faith' will be used as a metaphor to illustrate dimensions of faith that are supposed to work together but sometimes get overlooked or disconnected. Our hope in this series of books has been to promote what is called intentional or missionary discipleship. Looked at through the metaphor of the table, such discipleship has a number of interconnected dimensions, which can be distinguished although not separated. Initiating people into intentional or missionary discipleship must take place within this broader vision if the faith is to be whole and wholesome.

- *The reflected life*: This points to the personal journey of each one of us, the spiritual quest, the attempt to make sense of life. We hope to arrive at some integration of faith and life – through meditation, prayer, *lectio divina*, spiritual direction and so on.

- *Community of faith*: A privatised faith independent of the community of believers is a contradiction. At Baptism, we become members of an intentional, missionary community. The community sends us out and we return to the community. This belonging finds true expression in the shared Eucharist. We may for a while subsist somewhat independently, but in the long term this is far from ideal.

- *Understanding our faith*: It is the task of all of us to bring the faith into critical dialogue with the world around us.

Exploring the faith as adultstakes time and effort, but the end result should be a more life-giving integration of faith and our real lives.

- *Practical faith in our world*: This dimension encompasses a wide range, including personal conversion, ethical living and the struggle for justice in all its forms, including climate justice.

It is evident that distinguishing these dimensions is a work of analysis and therefore somewhat artificial. It is also probable that no one lives each dimension fully all of the time. In the normal course of events, at different stages in life, one or other aspect may achieve a greater prominence or importance. If any one of these dimensions is substantially missing or totally absent, for whatever reason, the experience of the faith will likewise be diminished and partial. To stay with the metaphor, the table will become unstable. Initiating people into missionary/intentional discipleship must, by its very nature, take account of all four aspects, however this is to be achieved. Such an integrated effort presumes that sacramental initiation takes place chiefly in the parish. The few observations added are an attempt to flesh out these ideas a little more fully.

THE TABLE OF THE FAITH

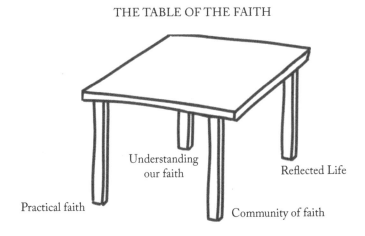

Understanding our faith

Reflected Life

Practical faith

Community of faith

Introduction

In the Synoptic Gospels – especially in Luke – we read of Jesus' practice of table fellowship. Jesus used meals to bring to expression the abundant and unfailing hospitality of the kingdom of God: all are welcome. From such accounts, we take the image of the table and we are going to use it to articulate important dimensions of faith and catechesis, especially in the Irish context. The Second Vatican Council picked up this imagery when it complemented the Table of the Eucharist with the Table of the Word.

Exploring the image

A table is a place for nourishment and refreshment, hospitality and welcome, friendship and communion. These words express a good deal of how we would like to be as a faith community. As we explore the image, we notice that a table stands and is steady when it has four supporting legs. Even if one support is missing or damaged in some way, a table will still be steady enough on three. However, if two legs are gone or not functioning fully, the table will be radically unstable and unable to bear its weight.

The 'legs' of the table of the faith are four: reflected life, community, understanding and service. By 'reflected life', we mean the spiritual engagement of each individual, on his or her own pilgrimage of faith. By 'community belonging', we mean being part of a real community of faith, where we find our own experiences and insights confirmed, discerned and challenged. By 'understanding', we mean the appropriate adult grasp of the faith, commensurate with education in other fields. 'Service' really means practical discipleship, including personal transformation and action for justice in our world.

The Irish 'Table of the Faith' was traditionally strong in some respects. To stay with the imagery, in the now somewhat distant past, devotions nourished the lives of the people and personal prayer was very much part of being Catholic. Likewise, Mass attendance – the chief expression of community belonging – was strongly embedded in the culture. In the same way, action for justice – often focused towards the developing world, but not exclusively – was strong. A traditional weakness would have been adult faith development. One somewhat unstable 'leg' meant the table still functioned quite well. This is no longer the case.

Without peering into people's lives, it looks as if the personal journey aspect has generally weakened and the practice of private prayer has lessened. Community belonging – at least as expressed in Mass attendance – is no longer what it was. We may say that the shell of such practice survives for events such as Christmas or First Holy Communion, but that the shell is increasingly perceived as hollow. Adult faith formation is often spoken about and promoted, but in real terms it is not reaching many people. One effect is that when people move away from the faith, they often don't really know why *and they don't miss it.* Perhaps the strong leg is still action for justice. On a humanitarian level, Ireland is still a generous society, not only towards the developing world but also internally. Even so, this may not necessarily come from faith, as such. All of this means that the Table of the Faith has become radically unstable, with only one, perhaps two, supports fully functioning.

Reflected Life

The human quest for meaning is a lifelong journey. This is true also for Christian life, rooted in a personal relationship with Jesus Christ. There are, then, many dimensions to the Christian journey:personal prayer, hearing the Word of God, attentiveness to the Lord, openness to the power of God's Spirit,discerning the movements of consolation and desolation, the things taking us to God, the things taking us from God.We recognise many of these elements when we come together to celebrate the Eucharist.

Mature faith also involves an integration of that faith with life. Individuals often benefit from support on their spiritual search – to be able to reflect on their experience with the eyes of faith. Discernment, spiritual direction, the wisdom of an Anam Cara, being part of faith group, all enable people to take ownership of their faith journey and to trust in their own inner wisdom.

Community of faith

As we know, being human is 'being-with-others', and our human experience of belonging is essential for our well-being. When our 'being-with-others' works well, it is hugely enriching and, as we know, when it falls short the harm can be great. As always, being a Christian builds on being human. For example, baptism invites us to become members of the community of faith, rooted in our experience of being part of a natural family.

Being a Christian is not easy today and it would be true to say that keeping faith alive alone is less and less feasible. We need the support, affirmation, celebration, critique and discernment that we find with fellow believers. Christianity is by nature convivial, in the literal sense of 'lived with others'.

Understanding our faith

As identified above, a traditional weakness of Irish Catholicism has been inadequate adult catechesis. It is commonly observed that people's education in the faith does not usually keep pace with their development in nearly every other area of life. Surviving into adulthood with a child's grasp of the issues is surely a recipe for disaffection and departure. We know from experience that many leave the wonderful adventure of the faith without any apparent sense of loss. We remember too that the special genius of Catholic Christianity is the conviction that truth is one and that faith and reason do not finally contradict each other. A critical appropriation and grown-up owning of the faith is part of what it means to be Catholic. How can this be achieved?

As the Table of the Faith would suggest, understanding is but one aspect of the entire project of believing. It cannot take the place of spirituality or service, for example. However, it is an important part of the integration of faith and life. Without this integration, our faith is fragmented and cannot be considered whole.

People often start exploring the faith by looking at the Bible. This is an excellent place to start: it is personal; it brings us in touch with Christ; it links with the Sunday liturgy. It is also very close to the increasingly popular practice of *lectio*. Biblical formation can take place at various levels of sophistication – from simple introductory presentations to degree courses offered online or by distance learning providers, and all the possible variations inbetween. There are also really good study editions of the Bible available as well as excellent introductions. Following recent Catholic teaching, establishing the meaning at the time of writing using the Historical Critical Method is itself critical. It is – does it need to be affirmed? – not the only way to read and of itself incomplete. In part, this is because we read the Bible not for historical information about the past but precisely for faith.

Because we read for faith, contemporary issues arise for discussion and, almost inevitably, participants find themselves asking theological questions that require theological responses. What is God really like? Who is Jesus? Where is the Spirit today?

Fortunately, we live at a time in which it is easier than ever to communicate and learn. As in the past, when the Church embraced the latest 'technology' (printed books), today we need to make full use of online resources and the IT revolution.

Practical faith in our world

At stake here is a very wide range of activities and expressions of the faith. The starting point is always my own continued personal conversion to Jesus and the Good News. There is no end point, but it should certainly include social justice and climate justice. This can be lived in the neighbourhood, in wider society or in more global action. The voices of the prophets are still powerful and their voices are loud when it comes to social justice. This is a favourite text of mine and it may help to remember that it is God (!) who is speaking:

> I hate, I scorn your festivals,
> I take no pleasure in your solemn assemblies.
> Your oblations, I do not accept them
> and I do not look at your communion sacrifices of fat cattle.
> Spare me the din of your chanting,

let me hear none of your strumming on lyres,
let justice flow like water,
and uprightness like a never-failing stream!

(Amos 5:21–24, New Jerusalem Bible)

The final couplet says it all. Directly inspired by such prophetic witness, the Gospel of Luke offers us this emblematic tableau:

> When Jesus came to Nazareth, where he had been brought up, he went to the synagogue on the sabbath day, as was his custom. He stood up to read, and the scroll of the prophet Isaiah was given to him. He unrolled the scroll and found the place where it was written:

> 'The Spirit of the Lord is upon me,
> because he has anointed me to bring good news to the poor.
> He has sent me to proclaim release to the captives
> and recovery of sight to the blind,
> to let the oppressed go free,
> to proclaim the year of the Lord's favour.'

> And he rolled up the scroll, gave it back to the attendant, and sat down. The eyes of all in the synagogue were fixed on him. Then he began to say to them, 'Today this scripture has been fulfilled in your hearing.' (Luke 4:16–21)

The Christian faith calls us work for justice in all its forms, in our personal lives, in our society, in our world, and, not least, in our Church.

For an integrated appropriation of the faith, all four dimensions identified here should be in place. Or, to change metaphors, a believer – to be fully engaged – needs to inhabit all four areas of faith. In reality, we grow as believers all the time and at different moments different aspects will be more alive than others. At the same time, the Table of the Faith provides a grid against which it is possible to assess where we are as individuals, as members of faith groups and even as Church, within contemporary society. As we travel together (*synodia*), towards the national assembly, perhaps such a grid may help us to recognise where we have come from ('a here') to where we are going ('a there').

Soli Deo Gloria!

Biblical Index

The index follows the order of Old Testament books as found in Catholic Bibles; the chapter and verse numbering follows the New Revised Standard Version.